The Well-Balanced
Family

*Reduce screen time and
increase family fun, fitness
and connectedness*

ROBERT F MYERS, PhD

CHILD PSYCHOLOGIST

Printed in the United States of America
10 9 8 7 6 5 4 3 2 1

Published By
Book Baby
7905 N. Crescent Blvd.
Pennsauken, NJ 08110

Print ISBN: 978-154396-104-1
eBook ISBN: 978-1-54396-105-8

Imprint
Parenting Today, LLC
www.parentingtoday.com

Please visit **parentingtoday.com/tools** for free full-size PDF versions of the tools provided in this book.

Library of Congress Control Number: 2019903143

CONTENTS

DEDICATION

I dedicate this book to my family. I thank you for all the fun times we shared with each other while growing as individuals and as a family. Now that we are all adults it's awesome to be connected in a way that we continue to enjoy being with each other often and can still play together as we continue to develop our ability to openly communicate and support each other. I love you all so much.

Robert Myers, PhD
2019

ACKNOWLEDGEMENTS

Thank you to Monica Foley for all her help with editing and providing valuable suggestions for content and to Nathan O'Leary for design and creative input. Photos from Shutter Stock.

PREFACE & HOW TO
USE THIS BOOK

THIS BOOK IS MEANT to be a guide to help families cut back on all forms of screen time. Reducing the use of digital devices will help promote positive habits for everyone in the family, resulting in an improvement in physical and mental health, organizational skills, and academic achievement. Taking advantage of the time made available will also lead to an increase in the experience of joy and community, both as individuals and as a family. I will present evidence on why this is of value as well as suggestions for behavior change based on research studies and recommendations provided by professional organizations and government agencies. The book will also provide suggestions on how children can use their digital devices safely while benefitting from the informational, entertainment and social benefits provided by this technology.

While I'll discuss some issues related to parenting and provide suggestions, this is not meant to be a parenting book. I'll offer tips to gain additional information on parenting from online resources and publications. This book is also not about digital device addiction. I'll present information on the harmful effects of overuse of electronic devices, as well as advice on how to reduce utilization. I'll describe the warning signs and give suggestions on how to seek help if you believe you or someone else in your family needs support. I'll provide recommendations for encouraging reading and reducing homework hassles, as well as resources for assistance with other education issues.

Finally, I'll present information related to improving health through increased exercise, stress reduction and better sleep habits, including health resources.

I hope you and your family will learn to spend more time playing and having fun while improving your ability to relate to each other more, along with developing a better understanding and appreciation for one another. To improve the flow of this book, you'll notice that sometimes I'll interchange how I refer to children—nouns and pronouns that either refer to a girl or a boy. When I use the term 'parent,' I'm referring to anyone who's involved in raising children in the home.

Suggestions for Using this Book

1. Start by reading through the entire book.

2. Once all parents and/or caregivers have read the book, meet and discuss how you would like to move forward as a family to implement the recommendations.

3. Next go to Chapter 16 and start your family meetings.

4. Decide as a family how to implement the suggestions related to screen time in Chapter 17.

5. Begin planning family activities.

6. Continue to discuss and implement other concepts such as fitness programs and organization strategies.

7. I suggest you periodically review the content of Sections 2 & 3 and discuss your progress in implementing these concepts into your relationship and your parenting. I highly recommend getting the recommended books for these chapters to expand your understanding of these concepts as well as get additional tools for your parenting toolkit.

8. The summary at the end of each of the four sections provide step-by-step suggestions for implementing the concepts as well as tools in the form of charts. [For full-size PDF versions of the charts and

other tools please go to parentingtoday.com/tools to download your free copy].

9. The Resources section provides links to government, nonprofit, and professional organization websites providing additional free information on the topics covered in each chapter. You will also find recommendations for books and other tools available on the internet.

Please be sure to visit parentingtoday.com/tools for PDF versions of the charts provided at the end of each section as well as additional resources, including updates, classes, and forums for parents.

CHAPTER 1

The Importance of a Well-Balanced Family in Today's World

Introduction

I BEGAN THINKING ABOUT the need for families to work on achieving a balance in daily activities after reading the latest guidelines on the use of media by children, which was published by the *American Academy of Pediatrics* (AAP) in November 2016. Previously, the recommendations focused on the amount of screen time that is appropriate for each developmental stage, as well as the age-appropriate selection of content. These guidelines continue for children under the age of six. For older children and adolescents, the AAP took a broader approach—looking at the need for balance in how they spend their time each day. The guidelines stressed the need for kids and teens to spend an adequate amount of time daily on the following:

- Exercising
- Engaging in play activities that don't involve electronics
- Spending time with other members of the family
- Sleep

The AAP even developed the Family Media Plan, a useful tool available at *www.healthychildren.org*. This resource helps families schedule and create goals around the amount of time that each member of the family spends watching TV, using a computer, tablet, smartphone, or playing video games.

Seeing the word 'family' in the title instead of 'children' reinforced for me the concept of how important the family is in the life of a child. During my years as a child psychologist, one fact that became clear to me is that you can't treat the child without also working with the family unit.

For example, a recent study of children's screen time found that a parent's screen time use had a significant impact on their child's use. Further analysis indicates that a child's screen time appears to be the result of the interaction between a child and their parent, which is further influenced by parental attitudes. Studies on other habits, such as diet and exercise, have also found that parental actions are a significant influence on the behavior of children and adolescents. Thus, a well-balanced approach to these habits and more should benefit every member of the family.

The emphasis on increasing other activities to reduce screen time is consistent with what we know about changing behavior—the best way to eliminate an undesirable behavior is to replace it with a more desirable one. Consistently practicing the new behavior builds habit strength while the old behavior weakens. Gradually, the new habit takes over, which is reinforced by the positive outcome it produces.

All members of a family benefit when the dynamic is one of sharing life and providing support for each other. Children and teens need parents that give love unconditionally, along with guidance and encouragement. This not only helps kids to grow and develop, but it promotes a family life full of mutual love and respect. Such an environment can result in additional benefits, including reduced stress and a healthier lifestyle. Given the recent increase in anxiety and depression among children and teens, a well-balanced family would serve as a preventative measure. This lifestyle promotes a positive self-concept to achieve success and the necessary resiliency to handle difficult situations when they occur.

I've been in practice as a psychologist since 1980 and primarily worked with children, teens and their families. During this time, I've observed three major developments that have had an impact on families:

1. Increased workload and hours for workers in the United States.

2. Increased emphasis on academics in education, from preschool to high school.

3. Increased use of electronic devices and digital media.

Today, quite a few adults are working more than one job to make ends meet, while others are working longer hours. Some employees today work almost 24/7, as they are tethered to their workplace by their cell phones and other electronic devices. While at home, in the car, or out and about, employees receive a constant flow of emails, phone calls, and texts, and are expected to drop everything and respond. The lack of sufficient sick days, vacation, and family leave also impact the amount and the quality of time they can spend with their families. This also cuts into their time for relaxation, recreation, sleep, and exercise.

The number of applicants to college has increased. This has caused the acceptance rate— especially for the top universities—to decrease significantly. Many parents feel that their child needs to get a degree from a top university to be successful this has resulted in parents keeping kids busy in tutoring, music lessons, volunteer activities, prepping for entrance exams, being involved in sports and other competitions. Because of recent federal legislation, the push by schools to get top rankings in math and reading scores has resulted in less free-play time in preschool and less recess and exercise time in elementary and high school. A "hurried" or "over-scheduled" lifestyle leaves little time for family activities reducing the time spent in the valuable experience of play for younger kids and less time for exercise and relaxation for older kids.

Finally, the rapid development of digital technology and social media has cut into time for family, exercise, and relaxation for children and adults alike. Electronic devices intrude on quality family time and communication between family members. It's not uncommon for kids and adults to engage in media multitasking, such as watching TV while texting. I also see more families out for dinner with the parents busy on their cell phones while the children are playing on their tablets—nobody is talking. Studies show there is less interaction in the home as well, despite research indicating that younger children don't learn as much from the use of educational apps as they do through communication with parents.

Research also reveals that excessive screen time is a significant factor in the rate of obesity in children and teens, interferes with sleep, and increases the likelihood of using alcohol and tobacco. Teens are more likely to engage in adverse activities such as cyberbullying, sexting, or becoming victims of online predators.

The Key Elements for Building a Well-Balanced Family

My goal in writing this book is to provide you with ideas and tools that will help you to build a family lifestyle that promotes the well-being of all members. Hopefully this leads to great times together that will instill a lifetime of fond memories and long, enduring family ties. Based on research and both my professional and personal experiences, I suggest that the key elements for a well-balanced family are:

- Connectedness
- Open Communication
- Healthy Living
- Organization

Connectedness creates a sense of belonging and feeling safe and secure. The basics include engaging in fun and meaningful activities, creating moments of close personal one-on-one time, developing family traditions, and providing personal space when needed. Reading with your children is also another way to stay connected as well as improve academic skills and open communication.

Open Communication results in each family member feeling loved and respected. It also makes it easier to handle conflicts when they arise. The basics include listening, empathy, supportive communication, and collaborative problem-solving.

Healthy Living is achievable in a well-balanced family by taking the following steps: developing a family agreement on screen time and phone time, committing to family mealtime, and working together as a team to promote personal fitness and a healthy lifestyle. This includes getting plenty of sleep and eating nutritiously and responsibly.

Organization happens when a family works together to develop a plan to achieve these goals. For it to be effective, all members of the family need to provide input, and the plan should be developed collaboratively with the acknowledgment that the adults have the final say. The process includes:

- Preparing a family mission statement
- Scheduling family meetings
- Establishing family routines
- Holding open but age-appropriate discussion of family finances
- Creating a plan to address homework and school issues

Throughout this book, I'll present a general approach on how to adapt the concepts for your family, as well as provide "how-to" lists of ideas and tools you can use. In a resources section at the end of the book, I'll also share online resources for more information, as well as a list of recommended books for further reading.

Based on current research, implementing the concepts and strategies will not only improve family life, but your efforts will also improve the health and wellness of all members of your family. Decreasing screen time and substituting with some of the recommended activities (including creative playtime and reading) will promote the development of language, problem-solving skills, and cognitive functioning. Using the approaches presented for improving communication and interpersonal relationships improves social skills, self-confidence, the ability to empathize and emotional regulation. Finally, engaging in family activities at home and the community develops character and social responsibility.

Getting Started

Covered in the book are the key elements outlined above in order of importance from a sense of psychological and physical wellbeing. My suggestion for the reader is to read or at least skim through the entire book. The starting point for implementation, however, should begin with Chapter 16 regarding establishing regular family meetings. At first family meeting or two, each family can decide their overall goals as well as individual goals. You can then move to develop a family agreement related to screen time as well as start a family activity schedule to promote spending more time together having fun and becoming more active.

CHAPTER 2

The Time Has Come to Strike a Balance in Our Use of Digital Devices

DIGITAL TECHNOLOGY HAS PRODUCED many new avenues for us to be entertained and informed as well as stay in touch with others. It wasn't long ago that screen time was limited to TV and movies. Communication was either in person, by telephone or by writing and mailing letters. Digital technology has also provided tools to increase our productivity at work and school, as well as made it more accessible and often less costly to acquire goods and services.

There's no doubt that our smart televisions, cell phones, tablets, computers, and game boxes have enriched our lives in many ways. However, research along with personal observation has led many of us to realize that as with any other activity, the use of these incredible tools can become "too much of a good thing." For the last few years, professionals in healthcare, education, and the social sciences have stressed the need to find a balance.

Today, more than 95% of US households own a mobile device. The use of mobile devices by children under the age of eight is almost ten times higher than it was in 2011. The latest Common Sense Media survey found that children under two years of age spend about 42 minutes per day using digital media, children two to four spend 2 hours and 39 minutes per day, and children five to eight spend 2 hours and 56 minutes using these devices. The survey also noted that since their previous study in 2013, the use of mobile devices by kids from zero to eight tripled, while the overall use of all types of media was about the same (2017, Common Sense Media, commonsensemedia.org).

In a nationwide study, the Kaiser Foundation found that children ages eight to eighteen spend an average of 7 hours and 38 minutes a day using various digital media devices, including 4.5 hours watching TV/videos, 1.5 hours on the computer, and over 1-hour playing video games. The study also found that this age group spends only 25 minutes per day reading (2010, *Generation M2: Media in the Lives of 8 to 18-Year-Olds*, kff.org). Adults spend over 12 hours per day watching major media, with about 5 hours of that time using digital devices (eMarketer.com 2015).

Social media use has also increased. According to *Social Media Today*, the average person will spend two hours per day on social media (YouTube, Facebook, Snapchat, Instagram and Twitter) and up to 45 minutes per day messaging. They report that teens spend up to 9 hours per day on social media (data for years 2012-2015 published in 2017 by socialmediatoday.com).

Some Good Reasons to Limit Digital Media Use

Health Problems In a growing body of research, there is a correlation between **obesity** and excessive screen time for both children and adults. This is caused primarily by a decrease in physical activity due to sedentary behavior. Another cause is the influence of commercials promoting snacks, soft drinks, fast food, and sweetened cereals to name a few, which result in unhealthy dietary habits. Some also indicate that the consumption of snacks and soft drinks relates to watching TV. The research not only suggests that these behaviors increase the rate of obesity, but also increase type two diabetes and cardiovascular disease.

Research studies have shown that decreasing TV time reduces both weight gain and a lower body mass index (BMI). Reducing video game use and replacing it with outdoor game time will not only help reduce the likelihood of weight gain. It will also prevent below normal serum levels of Vitamin D, which is now seen more frequently in children and adolescents.

As an example of the trend to more time spent with video games and less time playing outdoor games, I've noticed a change in the choice of topics on the Essay Competency section of the Wechsler Individual Achievement Test (WIAT). The task asks the child or adolescent to write an essay about their favorite game. For years, I would see written pieces on physical sports or sometimes a board game or card game. Now kids usually ask, "Is it okay to write about my favorite video game?"

Sleep Deprivation has also been linked to screen time. All electronic devices, including TV, cell phones and tablets emit blue light from the screen—which the brain interprets as sunlight and issues a signal to wake up. Many health professional organizations recommend that screen use of any type should cease at least 30 minutes before bedtime.

Research also indicates that children and teens who have electronic devices in their bedrooms get less sleep than those who don't. I've heard many times about kids getting back on their devices after bedtime and spending hours engaged with their iPads or iPhones. Sleep deprivation is another cause of obesity. Furthermore, it results in impairments in attention and concentration, problem-solving skills and emotional regulation (can we say crankiness). Adults are affected in similar ways. They often get out the last emails or texts before they go to bed and sleep next to a cellphone that remains turned on throughout the night.

Vision Problems are now sometimes correlated with excessive screen use. Both eye strain and eye pain are attributable to long periods of staring at the screen. According to *Web MD*, excessive screen time can result in "Computer Vision Syndrome," with symptoms including dry or red eyes, blurred or double vision, and headaches. Vision professionals frequently mention the 20-20-20 rule as one way to help prevent this. It calls for looking away from the screen every 20 minutes or so and looking at something at least 20 feet away for 20 seconds. Of course, cutting back on screen time and engaging in other activities such as exercise, working on a hobby, listening to music, or reading is also helpful. While extended time reading books can cause eye strain, it's less harmful because of the lack of glare and flicker from screen use. One of my favorite ways to read is by listening to a book while taking a walk.

Aches and Pains have been associated with the use of digital devices as well. I've actually experienced thumb pain from spending too much time scrolling on my cell phone. Neck and wrist pain can also occur due to holding them in awkward positions for extended periods of time. Associated with more severe conditions and the excessive use of various electronic devices are migraines, back pain, repetitive motion syndrome, and even arthritis.

Psychosocial Problems

Social Skills Development can be delayed due to children spending less time in face-to-face interactions with children and adults. When I ask some kids or teens how many friends they have, they may say, "I have at least ten friends I spend lots of time with almost every day." When I ask who they are, where they hang out, and what they do for fun, it's not uncommon for these kids to say, "Oh, we play video games together online, or we spend hours texting or chatting on our cell phones." In an experimental study on the effect of screen time and social skills, researchers at UCLA found that children who went for just five days without any screen time were better at reading human emotions than other children (October 2014, *Computers in Human Behavior*). Social isolation is becoming more frequent among children and teens. Lack of spending time engaging with others can lead to inadequate or inappropriate social skills, resulting in rejection and/or teasing by peers.

Increase in Negative Social Interaction has been connected to the intensive and inappropriate use of social media platforms. Cyberbullying has been increasing for several years among teens and is now seen more frequently in younger children as well. This activity can lead to serious consequences including anxiety and/or depression. When this behavior is intense and affects an already vulnerable kid, it can lead to physical aggression or even suicidal thoughts or behavior. Sexting by teens is also on the rise and creates its own set of problems. Children and teens need education about these dangers and how to protect themselves. Parents and educators should not only provide information and guidance but supervision as well.

Verbal and Physical Aggression in children and adolescents in some cases can be attributed to viewing programs with violent content or playing video games with violent and aggressive themes. Below are several examples of experimental studies that examined the connection between exposure to violent media content and human behavior.

A research study with preschoolers randomly divided the children into three groups. One group watched a "Batman and Superman" cartoon, the second watched an episode of "Mr. Rogers' Neighborhood," and the third group watched a show that did not have either a negative or positive message. Following the videos, the first group engaged in more aggressive play themes, even breaking toys and getting into fights. In contrast, the second group played more cooperatively and were more likely to help the teacher (December 2003, *Psychological Science in the Public Interest*). Young children, in particular, tend to imitate speech and behavior they have observed.

Published in the same issue of the journal cited above, a study with college students involving the exposure to movies with scenes of sexual violence found that this group, compared to a group viewing neutral films, found rape to be less serious of a crime. This is reflective of desensitization toward violent behavior, including lack of sympathy for the victims following brief exposure to violent programs.

There have been reports that some younger children exposed to violence on TV may become more fearful of their surroundings. This is seen in increased generalized anxiety as well as resistance to going to public places. I remember back in the early 1980's seeing a child who had become extremely anxious and had difficulty falling asleep and being afraid to be in public places. The sudden onset of these symptoms was a puzzle to his parents and at first to me.

During our therapy sessions, I discovered that he had seen a commercial for a "Freddy Krueger" movie broadcast during a late afternoon children's TV show. Even though his parents monitored their child's viewing carefully, this exposure to violence unfortunately occurred.

Some kids are influenced more easily than others. The research on this particular topic comes with mixed results. Parents need to be actively involved in guiding the viewing habits of younger children in particular. They should also be aware of the ratings of video games published by the Entertainment Software Ratings Board (ESRB). Additionally, websites such as *commensensemedia.org* and *kids-in-mind.com* provide evaluations of various media platforms and guide parents on media use and safety.

Depression in adolescents has been linked to the use of screens for activities including gaming, Internet, texting, and social media. One study found that teens who spent five or more hours using electronic devices were twice as vulnerable for depression and suicidal thoughts than their peers who spent only one hour per day on their phones.

Another longitudinal study discovered that individuals who reported more television time and more use of digital media, in general, were more likely to experience depressive symptoms as young adults. The participants did not report any depressive symptoms at the beginning of the study, but those with more media involvement reported significant depression symptoms at the 7-year follow-up assessment (February 2009, *American Archive of General Psychiatry*).

Teens who spend considerable time on social media are also more vulnerable to cyberbullying. Exposure to cyberbullying often leads to symptoms of anxiety and/or depression. In some cases, this can lead to severe symptoms, including school avoidance or suicidality. Parental guidance and monitoring of social media use, as well as other forms of digital communication by their teens, is recommended. A strong bond and having open communication will facilitate this process.

Teens who become depressed may visit websites regarding suicidality, some of which may increase the likelihood of suicide rather than result in a decrease. Suggestions for helping kids reduce screen time, using parental controls for computers, phones, and tablets as well as information on teaching kids about cyber safety are in Chapter 17.

Impact on Learning and Academics

A study of over 4,500 U.S. children (eight to eleven years of age) from across the country revealed that limiting recreational screen time to less than 2 hours per day, along with getting sufficient physical activity (1 hour per day) and the recommended amount of sleep (9-11 hours per day based on age) resulted in improved cognitive functions when compared to children who did not achieve any of these goals. However, children who adhered to only the screen time recommendation showed improvement in cognitive functioning, though not as significant as those who met both the screen time and sleep recommendations.

While iPads and other devices such as smartphone apps, educational television shows, and websites are used increasingly at home and in the classroom for learning, research indicates that time spent reading books results in improved brain connectivity between the visual word recognition area of the brain and the language and cognitive control regions of the brain. In this study, the assessment tool was brain imaging techniques, and the children were between eight and eleven years old. The findings indicate that increased time reading and limiting screen time improves brain development and literacy. Chapter 9 provides suggestions on how to increase children's reading time and stresses the importance of parental involvement in the activity.

The availability of digital devices also interferes with homework productivity. Children and teens who are required by their schools to complete assignments online often sneak onto the Internet or game apps on their computer or iPad. We will provide recommendations on how to monitor and guide this use later in the book. In addition to this advice, I'll offer suggestions and tools for improving study time and learning.

Young children benefit more from hands-on learning through play and interaction with others. The recommendation of *California First Five* to read, talk and sing to your children every day is essential to intellectual, language and social development. Kids need exposure to toys as well as things around the house and in nature to stimulate curiosity and exploration, which results in positive growth and development. Screen time for children up to age five should be limited to no more than one hour per day. Even being exposed to "second-hand screen time," such as playing on the floor while the TV is on for the older people in the room has been associated with lower ability to attend and concentrate—not only at the time of the experience—but can result in shorter attention spans even when they are older.

Over the last two decades, new scientific technology has made it possible for neuroscientists to learn more about how the brain works. This has led to striking discoveries related to neuroplasticity. In the past, we believed that we had so many brain cells and that was it. Scientists have since learned that we continue to grow new nerve cells, and that nerve cells are continually developing new connections. This is especially true during child and adolescent development, but it continues throughout life.

Physical and mental activity, along with social interactions, are constantly rewiring the brain by either producing new brain cells or wiring them together. Learning to ride a bike or taking piano lessons results in developing new brain cells and connections. These connections occur when two or more brain cells fire at the same time. The saying in neuroscience that describes this process is "cells that fire together, wire together." We all know that once we have learned to ride a bike, we're still able to ride one even if we haven't for years. Maybe we're a little wobbly at first, but as soon as those neurons start firing, it all comes back.

First Five California is a program created by the passing of Proposition 10 in 1998 to develop and fund programs to promote healthy child development. One of the goals is to encourage parents to spend time and interact with their young children to nurture their developing brains. In California, we frequently see public service announcements on local television promoting, "Talk. Read. Sing. It changes everything." I would add "play" to that as well as encouraging physical activity and curiosity by exposing children to nature, culture, science and more.

While the first five years are a critical time for the development of motor skills, language and cognitive skills related to thinking and learning, it doesn't stop when your child goes to school. Parents are their child's first, most important, and valuable teachers. Spending time with children and adolescents—engaging them in conversation, playing and having fun together, exposing them to the world around them, promoting curiosity, encouraging them to try new things and helping them develop social skills and emotional regulation skills are paramount to kids growing up to become happy, friendly, productive adults.

Research and experience show us that limiting screen time—while increasing physical activity, sleep, social interaction, reading books, and play—improves health, development, learning, and enjoyment of life in children of all ages. The is the same for adults. The goal is not to trash all of our devices but find the right balance for all members of the family to achieve these goals while continuing to take advantage of new technology in a way that is reasonable, responsible, and balanced.

This book is not just about how to reduce the use of screen time for everyone in the family. It's about exchanging that time for activities that promote positive physical, mental and social-emotional development for all members of the family. It's about building healthy bodies and brains. It's about having fun and enjoying being with each other.

Positive bonding between parents and children which continues through adolescence results in kids who are eager to learn, engage in positive activities outside the home, and are high achievers academically and socially. Children and teens raised in this type of home environment are far less likely than their peers to abuse substances or engage in antisocial behavior. Adult benefits include improved physical and mental health and reduced stress, along with increased joy and personal satisfaction.

CHAPTER 3

The Myth of the Typical American Family

Changes in the Size and Shape of Families

THE NOTION THAT THERE is such a thing as the "typical American family" has been gradually fading. Early TV sitcoms usually depicted a nuclear family, comprised of two parents and their biological children. But that isn't the reality we live in anymore.

Today's American families are a broad mix, including single-parent families, blended families, unwed couples, same-sex couples, adoptive families, and children being cared for by their grandparents. In some families, one of the parents may be incarcerated, because unfortunately, the U.S. has the world's highest incarceration rate.

The New York Times reported on several population trends affecting the makeup of families in a recent article (2016, *The Changing American Family).* Some of the findings on evolving family demographics, which vary between socio-economic groups, include:

- Fewer women are becoming mothers, and those who do are having fewer children.

- More than 40 percent of American babies are now born to unmarried women, primarily women in their 20s and 30s.

- Marriage rates are now at historic lows. While divorce rates have fallen, they are still high (about 40 percent).

- Both men and women are getting married later in life.

- 30 percent of American families are now headed by single parents, either divorced, widowed or never married.

- The number of same-sex couples raising children has doubled in the last decade.

Other trends mentioned in the article include the tremendous increase in the number of mothers who are working either part-time or full-time. In fact, in more than two-thirds of American families, both parents work outside of the home. In many instances, the woman is the primary or only source of income for a family. There are also an increasing number of stay-at-home dads and fewer stay-at-home moms.

The Myth of the Perfectly Functioning Family

On the popular 1950's family sitcom "Father Knows Best," the father came home from work, swapped his suit and tie for casual pants and a sweater, and sat by the fire talking to his two children about their day. Meanwhile, the mother was busy preparing the evening meal in the kitchen. While the script did call for occasional conflicts between members of the family, they were always resolved intelligently, after a mostly calm discussion. There was a little yelling now and then, but most of the time things were calm. The families in these types of shows all came from middle to upper-middle class families, they were well dressed, well-fed, and lived in a large and comfortable home.

While current television shows typically portray more diverse families and slightly more realistic characters, the conflicts are still fairly tame–and most are still successfully resolved within 30 to 60 minutes. Even today, many parents and kids unfavorably compare their family life to what they see on TV shows, such as how these fictional families regularly enjoy time with each other and can relate to one another with minimal conflicts.

The truth is that harmony does not always abound in families. Parents have moments of disagreement or may take their daily stress and frustrations out on each other. Siblings taunt one another, fight over the use of a toy or electronic device or try to get each other in trouble. Families are so busy with day-to-day living, getting homework done and spending time on the Internet or social media that they aren't making time for family fun. Many families also experience considerable financial stress as well, which affects all members of the family.

As humorist Emma Bombeck put it: "The family. We were a strange little band of characters trudging through life sharing diseases and toothpaste, coveting one another's desserts, hiding shampoo, borrowing money, locking each other out of our rooms, inflicting pain and kissing to heal it in the same instant, loving, laughing, defending, and trying to figure out the common thread that bound us all together."

What Is a Family and How Can a Family Work for All Its Members?

In general, a family is a group of people who share a common legal, and in most cases, blood bond. While the broader definition of a family is constantly evolving, some basic components comprise the experience. The family shares a similar set of experiences, and at least partially shares a set of values, beliefs, and traditions. Ideally, a family also provides an environment that is non-judgmental and offers unconditional love and support.

We should also acknowledge that each of the adult members of a family, as well as any children who come to the family through adoption or a re-marriage, bring their own experience as members of their family of origin. These are likely to include both positive and negative experiences, and sometimes differing values and expectations. Consciously and openly exploring this amalgamation of experience, perception, behaviors, emotions, and preconceived notions are the key to being able to form a family experience that works for all.

According to Virginia Satir, a well-known family therapist, "Feelings of worth can flourish only in an atmosphere where individual differences are appreciated, mistakes are tolerated, communication is open, and rules are flexible–the kind of atmosphere that is found in a nurturing family."

Key Components of a Well-Functioning Family

Parents should have a realistic expectation of themselves, including their unique set of abilities and the availability of time and money. When determining how we would like to live as a family and raise our children, we need to be fair in evaluating our progress and see things in their proper context.

Each child should be seen and accepted as a unique individual who is ever-changing as a result of the process of development and maturation. Children are all born with temperamental traits that may determine whether they're viewed as "easy" or "difficult" to raise. Every child also has a unique set of talents, as well as physical and intellectual strengths and weaknesses. While education, guidance, training, and encouragement may enhance the more desirable traits while minimizing some less desirable ones, each child should feel understood, and encouraged to become the best they can be.

A sense of humor is a sign of a well-functioning family, as well as a habit of engaging in fun activities together. When possible, families should develop shared interests, mutual goals, and devote time to participating in related activities, including hobbies and recreational activities.

There should be clear rules that ALL family members are expected to follow. Families should work together to establish routines that lead to the smooth functioning of daily living.

Don't approach parenting with the attitude of, "Do as I say, not as I do." One research study after another documents how children's behavior is profoundly affected by the actions of their parents.

Parents also need to allocate time and attention to take care of their own physical, mental or spiritual needs. This means that couples should plan occasional getaways together, as well as individually. Single parents also need to find ways to spend time away from home both on their own as well as with supportive friends and family in their life.

It's important not to attend to other family members' needs before your own. Just like they tell you during the pre-flight airline safety spiel, you should always "Secure your own oxygen mask before helping the person next to you."

Parents should routinely schedule one-on-one time with each child. It doesn't have to involve something elaborate either. It can be as simple as taking your child with you when you're running errands, having lunch together, reading to them, saying individual night-time prayers and finding opportunities to talk to them where it's free from the distraction of others. In families with more than one parent, you should also switch it up, so moms are spending time with sons, and dads with daughters, not just the sometimes more natural same-gender relationships.

Families tend to be more isolated these days due in part to busy schedules and physical distance from one another. To help combat the potential isolation, families should embrace available support from extended family, and their community. Spending time with other family members can strengthen existing familial bonds and create the opportunity to engage in fun and meaningful activities with relatives other than immediate family members. Children can benefit from individual time with other adult family members, as well as share fun times with cousins. Religious institutions and other community organizations, such as scouting, can also provide additional elements of support to families.

Working on developing and maintaining a well-functioning family will take time and effort from everyone in the family—it won't happen overnight. But if you commit to the process, you'll gradually see progress. Over a period of time, it will start to feel more natural and routine.

Ideally, you'll find that everyone in the family will come to appreciate this process and actively participate, and hopefully you'll all have fun and grow together.

SECTION 1 –
Connectedness

Connectedness creates a sense of belonging and feeling safe and secure. The basics include engaging in fun and meaningful activities, creating moments of close personal one-on-one time, developing family traditions, and providing personal space when needed.

Chapter 4: Connectedness Is a Top-Down Process

Chapter 5: The Importance of Play in the Lives of Children & Families

Chapter 6: Family Traditions & Family Activities

Chapter 7: Connecting with Your Kids

Chapter 8: Personal Space

Chapter 9: Family Reading Time

CHAPTER 4

Connectedness is a Top-Down Process

WHEN I USE THE term "connectedness," I'm referring to parent-child connectedness. Connectedness is the mutual emotional bond between parents and children that lasts over time. When the level of connectedness in a family is high, we see increased levels of affection, warmth, satisfaction, and trust with minimal conflict. When this is present in a family, parents and kids enjoy spending time with each other, they share similar values and have a positive outlook on life. They have open communication, share a mutual respect and support each other. This starts with the bonding between a newborn and parents but continues to develop when parents can build on this by taking the time and effort to grow and develop their relationship with each child. Recent research has shown that parent-child connectedness serves as a protective factor. It seems to help prevent the occurrence of several health and social problems in adolescents.

I'll be sharing several approaches to improving connectedness that you can build on throughout this book. In this chapter, the main point is that to increase the level of connectedness in a family—the parents need to be on the same page. Whether we're talking about the "traditional" family, single-parent family or blended family, the adults must possess a sense of inner-connectedness. This means they should have a sense of well-being and be free of either inner conflicts or conflicts with others involved in the parenting process.

If we're not fully aware of our own feelings and thoughts about parenting, they can creep into our child-rearing style without our knowledge. All of us carry into our role as parents the experiences we had in our formative years with relatives and others in the community, including teachers and peers. We internalize these experiences, and from time to time they will influence how we view various circumstances as well as how we behave in these situations.

When we've not sorted through our life experience and found elements that may have either a positive or negative effect on our thoughts and behavior, we tend to react to current situations without thinking things through. When we've examined our past, we can begin to make choices and respond to situations rather than react.

In reviewing your experience growing up, try to go back and look at your relationship with your parents and others who may have helped raise you with these questions in mind:

- What do you remember about your parents?

- What did you appreciate about the way they raised you?

- What difficulties or conflicts do you recall?

- How did they make you feel?

- Do they still come up and do they influence your thoughts and behavior?

- Do you remember your family as being accepting and supportive of you, or did you feel they were rejecting?

- How were you disciplined?

- Was there abuse or violence in the home?

- Were there others in your sphere of influence who provided love and support, such as relatives or teachers?

- If you could rewrite the story of your childhood, what would you keep and change?

- What kind of parent do you want to be?

- How were you treated by peers?

- Were you liked or were you bullied?

- Who were your best friends?

- What kinds of activities did you enjoy most?

- Think about significant events such as moving from one place to another, injuries or illnesses, school experience, accomplishments, disappointments, etc. How did they affect you, both positively and/ or negatively?

Once you've taken your own inventory, share it with someone you trust. If you're married or in a relationship, talk it through with your partner. Ideally, you both can share your experiences and then began to formulate a mutual notion on parenting. Think about how you can work together to develop a style that will create an atmosphere that will foster the characteristics associated with a family life that is high on parent-child connectedness.

Developing Your Parenting Style

Whether you're a single parent or a co-parent (sharing parenting duties with a spouse, significant other, friend, family member, ex-spouse, etc.), it's essential to develop a parenting style that works on fostering connectedness. Your parenting style began to evolve when you were a small child. How you were parented, your experiences growing up, and your values shape how you approach parenting. Your goals for your child and your definition of parenting success play an important role in your parenting style.

Your spouse comes to the role of parenting with his or her own experiences, beliefs, and values. Styles can often conflict. When two parents don't agree on how to raise their children, it isn't just difficult on a relationship; it's challenging for the children. But there is a light at the end of the tunnel. With an open heart and an open mind, the two of you can work together. If you're a single parent, view the information below as a way to help you be consistent in your parenting style and avoid outside influences that may interfere with your ability to parent effectively.

Understand Your Style

There are three different styles of parenting:

Authoritarian parenting entails strict rules and consequences. Authoritarian parents hold very high standards for their children. They follow their child very closely, checking grades, and when they attend sports or other activities, they often expect their child to be the best. At home, they set extremely exact rules for conduct and often require the completion of an excessive number of chores. When a child breaks the rules, they usually resort to punishment. If a child does not meet their high standards of performance in school and activities, they often put their kids down and tell them how disappointed they are in them. Authoritarian parents generally reserve praise for 100% achievement of their standards. They may hold their child to higher standards than they require of themselves. This parenting style often leads to a child with low self-esteem, feeling ashamed and becoming anxious and depressed–or one who becomes defiant and as they get older, they stay away from home as much as possible. Healthier responses on the part of children are seeking positives from other adults and becoming independent as soon as possible.

Permissive parenting usually derives from a parent wanting to be their child's "best friend." Permissive parents place few rules on their child and are quite lenient. Children require both love and limits–they need to have age-appropriate limits and boundaries. Having limits and boundaries makes a child feel more secure. A while back, a psychological experiment took place on a playground. The fence was removed around the playground. Without a fence, the children stayed close to the center of the playground–they didn't venture out to the perimeter. When the fence was replaced, the children would go up to the fence and look out. The fence provided a sense of safety and security. Children with parents who provide guidance and limits learn to respect others and can function in a wide range of environments and adapt to the norms. Children of permissive parents may feel loved, but they may have difficulty adjusting to rules and expectations set by leaders in settings outside their home.

Authoritative parenting also has rules and consequences. However, it's more responsive to a particular child's personality and needs. It relies on encouragement, coaching, rewards, logical consequences and sometimes natural consequences rather than punishment. Authoritative parents provide both love and limits—they're encouraging. When appropriate, these parents allow children to make choices. They teach and model appropriate social behavior. They provide praise frequently but don't "over-do it." They engage in mutual problem solving to resolve conflicts. When necessary, they may provide logical consequences such as, "when you finish your homework you may watch TV." An example for a teen could be, "because you came home late two times in a row, you will lose your car privileges for two weeks, and then you can try again at using the car responsibly."

Authoritative parents spend time talking with their children about their activities and their thoughts and feelings. They spend time playing with them and engaging in hobbies or other activities. When a child makes a mistake, the authoritative parent uses the occasion as a "teachable moment." They help the child to understand why their action was not in their best interest and help them learn to handle similar situations in the future more appropriately. Children then understand that "I made a bad choice, but I'm not a bad person." This high level of communication leads to connected kids and parents, and children who aren't afraid to admit mistakes. These children develop self-confidence and become responsible, confident, and empathetic adults.

Understanding where your style fits, and where your spouse's style fits, is the beginning. Many years of research has shown that beyond a doubt, the **Authoritative** parenting style is the most effective. The suggestion I give to the parents I see in my practice is for them to read books on parenting together, openly discuss their thoughts, and agree how to implement the material once they fully understand the concepts and strategies. [Please see my recommendations for books on parenting in the Resource section of the book for this chapter].

Communicate. Sit down and talk about how you and your partner each view your role as a parent to be. What are your goals? How do you define a successful parent? What values do you want to instill in your child, and how do you think you can help them grow up to be a successful adult? Talking will help both of you realize that while there may be differences, there are also similarities.

Create a Plan. Consider creating what you might call a parenting mission statement, which outlines the various areas that are important to you and your family, and what priorities you want to emphasize. For example, regarding education, what do you expect from your child? Creating a parenting plan is a document that you create together and gives you a template from which to work.

Establish a System That Supports Team Parenting. Agree on how you're going to approach parenting together. For example, small issues may be managed as they occur. However, larger discipline problems may be handled together after you've had a chance to discuss the situation.

Allow Room for Mistakes. Neither parent is perfect, and both will make mistakes. Blame, anger and conflict don't help either one of you, nor does it help your children. Keep parental conflict away from your children and discuss your differences calmly.

Finally, if you're struggling to agree, consider getting professional help. A parenting class or a counselor can help the two of you come together. It's possible for you to find common ground and parent even when your styles conflict. Be sure to read the resource guide at the end of this book to find more information on parenting and parenting style.

Use Mindfulness Techniques to Help You Implement Your Parenting Style Successfully

What Is Mindful Parenting? It seems that for every generation, there is a parenting trend or approach that is new. In 2009, Jon Kabat-Zinn, Ph.D., released a revised edition of his book, *Everyday Blessings: The Inner Work of Mindful Parenting,* co-written with his wife, Myla Kabat-Zinn. It was published in 1997. However, it wasn't until 2009 that the mindfulness approach began to take hold. To understand what mindful parenting is, it's essential first to understand what it means to be mindful.

What Does It Mean to Be Mindful? Mindful living, or the mindful approach, is about attempting to live and be in the moment–to experience each moment as it's happening. The tendency is for people to have constant chatter in their heads. You might be talking to your boss, but you're actually thinking about what you must do when you get home. To be mindful means that instead of thinking about what has happened, or what's going to happen, you're focused on what is happening right now. To be mindful means to slow down and become aware of your thoughts and feelings. It's a difficult practice, and many people meditate to train themselves to become more mindful.

Mindfulness as It Relates to Parenting. Mindful parenting strives to improve the moments you're with your child. When you're interacting with your child, the goal is to be 100 percent focused on them rather than thinking about what you're making for dinner, how you're going to find time for a shower or the fact that your child hasn't eaten any vegetables in the past 12 hours.

Mindful parenting also teaches parents to become less reactive to the trials and tribulations of parenting instead of allowing your emotions to dictate your response to a situation. For example, if your child hit your car with a rock, you're able to be aware of your thoughts and emotions and respond appropriately. You're able to approach each of your child's mistakes as a calm and in-control parent.

Is It Realistic? Mindfulness and becoming more aware of your thoughts and emotions is a powerful ability. And yes, when you're able to be completely present with your child, your interactions will be joyous and rewarding, even when they're misbehaving. However, practicing mindfulness 100 percent of the time is unrealistic. No one is perfect and being a parent is an emotional job. According to Kabat-Zinn, "Mindful parenting is not about being a yogi or practicing; it's about being human and realizing that we have more options than we may think in any moment, no matter what is happening."

You can begin to practice more mindful parenting right now. When you're experiencing an emotional reaction to your child, count to 10 and take deep breaths. As you interact with your child, enjoy the experiences. Don't allow outside influences, including thoughts and fears, to interrupt your time together.

Teaching Family Values to Your Family

Another way we can foster connectedness is to develop and impart a set of family values. It's easy to talk about instilling family values in your household, but how to do it can be a little confusing. However, it need not be difficult. With a few basic yet specific approaches and ideas, teaching family values can be incorporated into your everyday life.

What Are "Family Values?" Generally speaking, the term, "family values" usually refers to positive character traits such as honesty, forgiveness, respect, responsibility, patience, empathy and generosity. How these play out and what form they take varies from family to family.

For instance, one family might interpret "responsibility" as caring for the environment and taking responsibility for a clean neighborhood and healthy planet. In another family, responsibility may be more of a financial nature, referring to responsible money habits. And of course, it could mean both in the same family.

So how do you teach these things? First, think about what these values mean to your family. Does "honesty" mean never telling a lie? Or does it mean being up-front with your thoughts and feelings? What about patience–does that refer to delayed gratification, or being tolerant of others' quirks? Once you get an idea of how these values look in your family, you can begin instilling them. Here is some advice on how to do that.

Lead by Example. You may think your family isn't watching, but they are. If you're finding it hard to instill patience and tolerance in your kids, perhaps they see the opposite modeled in you. Do you have angry outbursts at other drivers when you're on the road? Do you get annoyed when your kids take too long to get ready to go somewhere? Maybe you're not generous with your time or money.

Take a look at your own behavior, and when you modify it, point it out. For example, you can say, "Oh, that person cut me off in this traffic! Normally I would get mad about that, but I'm choosing to keep calm. Maybe that person has a family emergency going on." This brings us to another vital family value: empathy.

Teaching Empathy. As in the example above, discuss possible and realistic scenarios for people's behavior. This will help your children to form those "pathways" in their brains so that when someone is frustrating, their minds may turn automatically to empathetic thoughts, such as, "Maybe she's having a bad day," or, "That person may be nasty because she lost a loved one recently."

Try to tie it in with your family's experiences. For example, you could say to your child, "Remember when you were really upset and didn't want to talk when your pet died? Maybe that person didn't talk to you because his pet just died."

A lot of family values come down to relationships with other people–treating people kindly, being honest and responsible with other's time, and so forth. The first relationship experiences we have are in our families. Therefore, leading by example and taking care to verbalize and explain how and why we act the way we do can go a long way toward making family values an integral part of your family members' lives.

Signs of Family Connectedness:

- Your family has regular family meetings.

- Your family checks in with each other about how they are feeling, how things are going in their life or in their day.

- Family members frequently share hugs with each other.

- You read together as a family.

- Your family discusses important issues, including family plans and decisions as well as current events in your community, organizations with which the family or family members associate, kids' sports, national or world news, sports and/or your favorite teams, weather, business and so on. Discussions on current events are at age-appropriate levels so all members of the family can participate.

- Your family discusses and exhibits shared values such as accepting each other's strengths and limitations, open and supportive communication, and dividing family responsibilities.

- You enjoy doing fun things together.

As you begin to understand and implement some of the recommendations shared throughout this book, you'll see more connectedness in your family. You'll feel good that your family continues to enjoy the warmth and support provided in this atmosphere, and you'll see that connectedness makes it easier to be a parent who guides and supports your children. You'll also notice that your children feel more self-confident, which is reflected in their personal achievements and their relationships with peers and adults. Finally, connectedness reduces sibling rivalry as well as parents feeling the need to nag or yell.

CHAPTER 5

The Importance of Play in the Lives of Children & Families

The Importance of Play in Child Development

MARIA MONTESSORI IS OFTEN quoted as saying, "Play is the work of a child." This is most certainly true. Jean Piaget, a child psychologist, devoted his life to studying how children learn and develop. He has referred to children as "little scientists." Through his observations of children in his laboratory and their natural environment, he found that children have an innate, natural curiosity which causes them to observe and interact with people and objects to learn how things work and behave, as well as how to communicate with them to achieve goals.

The role of the parent in fostering learning through play activities, as well as social interaction, is to provide what Lev Vygotsky, another developmental psychologist, referred to as "scaffolding." You may hear this term used by teachers. It means that adults can support learning just as scaffolding is used to provide temporary support for a building during the process of construction. Forms of scaffolding could be providing additional materials, giving advice, modeling a task, providing instruction, or encouraging a child to stay with a learning experience if he shows signs of frustration. In this role, the parent is serving as a coach. Of course, much of play is just for having fun and sharing the experience with others through social interaction. In that case, the parent is just another playmate. In this role, parents should sit back and enjoy. It's okay to let your child make up the rules for a game or direct you in a fantasy play situation.

The benefits of play are enumerated and explained in "The Power of Play: A Pediatric Role in Enhancing Development in Young Children," an article published in September 2018 in *Pediatrics*. Recent neuroscience research shows that play results in brain building. Play serves a vital role in all of the developmental domains, including cognitive, language, motor, social and emotional. Animal-based experimental research shows that play stimulates the production of BDNF (brain-derived-neurotrophic factor) which is essential to the growth and development of neurons (brain cells). One experiment involving rat pups found that two hours per day of play with objects resulted in positive changes in the weight of the brain and efficiency in problem-solving. Similarly, for children, researchers have found that children who engaged in one hour per day of active play were better at thinking creatively and multitasking than their peers in the control group. Other findings including time spent in active play with toys, was associated with enhanced attention, concentration, and cognitive flexibility.

Observation of play in a wide array of animals reveals its importance in social development. Other research found that play lowers levels of the stress hormone (cortisol) in animals, indicating that play may reduce stress. In fact, animals who were less stressed engaged in more active and more frequent play than animals with higher stress levels.

According to Dr. Stuart Brown, a leading expert on play who once studied seriously disturbed people who commit a crime, not having the opportunity for free play in childhood is often part of the life story of maladjusted individuals. Play is a "state of mind," says Brown, and "an absorbing, apparently purposeless activity that provides enjoyment and a suspension of self-consciousness and sense of time."

Get rid of play, and you'll measure a quickly-rising level of stress and negative outcomes. The move in some schools to replace recess with academic time threatens to chip away at a mid-day free play period that stimulates creativity, learning, and brain functioning, and in the long run, will work out poorly for the schools that try it.

Outdoor play usually involves some type of exercise which improves health in many ways including better sleep, healthier body weight, and cardiovascular health. Exposure to sunshine for at least one hour per day is essential for the body to produce sufficient levels of Vitamin D. Physicians are seeing a growing number of children and adolescents with a deficiency in this crucial vitamin.

How children play is also significant. Research has found that play with traditional toys such as blocks and dolls is more productive in developing their knowledge base, language skills, cognitive functioning, and social skills than using digital learning devices, playing electronic games or watching a video.

It's important for parents to know some basic facts and concepts on play and how it affects child development. Below, I will share some information from our website on the basics of play, including the purpose of play as well as play at various stages of development.

Forms of Play

As children develop, they will move from individual play to group play. How an older child chooses to play may depend on how they feel at the moment or could be a personal preference. The way most children play usually varies from day to day and situation to situation. There are three basic forms of play:

Solitary Play. Babies usually like to spend much of their time playing on their own. They are exploring all aspects of their environment from the sound of their own voice and the feel of their own body parts to those of others. They want to gaze upon, grab, suck and rattle any object that comes their way.

Older children at times will also prefer to play on their own. They may spend hours making up stories with their GI Joes or Barbie Dolls. They like to build, draw, paint, invent and explore by themselves. They hopefully will also like to read and even write on their own.

Parallel Play. From the age of two to about three, children move to playing alongside other children without much interaction with each other. They may be engaged in similar activities or completely different activities, but they like being around others their age. Even though it may appear that they don't care about the presence of other children, try separating them, and you will see this contact from afar is very important to them.

Group Play. By the age of three, children are ready for preschool. They're potty trained, able to communicate and socialize with others. They're able to share ideas and toys. Through interactive play, they begin to learn social skills such as sharing and taking turns. They also develop the ability to collaborate on the "theme" of the play activity. The children–not adults–should institute play themes and structure. Adults should only intervene when children exhibit the need for coaching on social and problem-solving skills.

Finally, children also like to play with adults. This can be one-on-one or in a group. It's important that parents spend time playing with their children–it's fun. Let the kids set the pace and become a part of their world. No need to teach or preach–just enjoy the experience.

Types of Play

Motor/Physical Play. Motor play provides critical opportunities for children to develop individual gross and fine muscle strength, as well as the overall integration of muscles, nerves, and brain functions. Recent research has confirmed the critical link between stimulating activity and brain development. Young children must have ample opportunities to develop physically, and motor play instills this disposition toward physical activity in young children.

Social Play. A variety of opportunities for children to engage in social play are the best mechanisms for progressing through the different social stages. By interacting with others in play settings, children learn social rules such as, give and take, reciprocity, cooperation, and sharing. Through a range of interactions with children at different social stages, children also learn to use moral reasoning to develop a mature sense of values. To be prepared to function effectively in the adult world, children need to participate in lots of social situations.

Constructive Play. Constructive play is when children manipulate their environment to create things. This type of play occurs when children build towers and cities with blocks, play in the sand, construct contraptions on the woodworking bench, and draw murals with chalk on the sidewalk. Constructive play allows children to experiment with objects; find out combinations that work and don't work; and learn basic knowledge about stacking, building, drawing, making music, and constructing. It also gives children a sense of accomplishment and empowers them with control of their environment. Children who are comfortable manipulating objects and materials also become good at manipulating words, ideas, and concepts.

Fantasy Play. With fantasy play, children learn to abstract, to try out new roles and possible situations, and to experiment with language and emotions. Additionally, children develop flexible thinking; learn to create beyond the here and now; stretch their imaginations, use new words and word combinations in a risk-free environment, and use numbers and words to express ideas, concepts, dreams, and histories. In an ever-more technological society, lots of practice with all forms of abstraction–time, place, amount, symbols, words, and ideas–is essential.

Games with Rules. Developmentally, most children progress from an egocentric view of the world to an understanding of the importance of social contracts and rules. Part of this development occurs as they learn that games such as *Follow the Leader*, *Red Rover*, *Simon Says*, baseball and soccer cannot function without everyone adhering to the same set of rules. The "games with rules" idea teaches children a critically important concept—the game of life has rules (laws) that we all must follow to function productively.

Play and Developmental Stages

Birth-18 months. Almost all neuron (nerve cells) are present at birth, but most aren't connected into networks. The connecting process (synapse formation) is rapid during this year, with brain activity becoming closer to an adult than a newborn by twelve months. Areas of greatest growth are sensorimotor, visual cortex, and later the frontal lobes. Play reflects the development of brain areas—this is what Piaget called "practice play."

Sight, sound, touch, taste, smell: these are the ways babies learn about the world and why the best infant toys are usually brightly colored noisemakers. They soon graduate from mobiles (try a musical one for extra interest) and mirrors (which they find fascinating) to grasping and holding. Toys they can manipulate with pleasing effects—activity quilts with different textures; attachments that squeak or jingle; rattles; activity bars: soft balls to drop and retrieve—begin to teach children dexterity and the concept of cause-and-effect.

As babies learn to sit up, crawl, stand, and then walk, the possibilities quickly expand. They're ready to experiment with nesting cups, activity boxes, stacking rings, large blocks, and a little later with shape-sorters. These toys help children develop fine motor skills and create relationships among objects. Cloth or board books, especially intriguing with pictures of faces or familiar objects, let them practice object-recognition and instill basic ideas of language. Babies and toddlers also love bathtub toys because they delight in all kinds of water play such as filling, emptying, and splashing. And as soon as they're up on their feet, they're ready to roll with push-pull toys.

A word of caution: Be sure any toy for a child in this age group has no small pieces that can be removed or broken off and swallowed, no sharp edges or points, and is made of non-toxic materials.

18 months-3 years. During this age, the synapses continue to expand and reach about 1,000 trillion—twice the density of the adult brain. (Pruning takes place later to reduce the number). The toddler's brain is twice as active as the adult brain. The structures of the brain that are sensitive to language and social-emotional response develop. Motor development continues at a rapid pace.

Action is the name of the game for toddlers, who delight in running, jumping, climbing and riding. A ride-on toy to zip around on will be a sure-fire hit, whether it's a low tricycle or a foot-to-floor vehicle in a whimsical bus or car design. Low climbing toys, large balls, and outdoor items such as a sandbox or wading pool are also good choices for developing gross motor skills.

Take-apart toys, pop-up toys, and simple puzzles gratify toddlers' curiosity about how things work, reinforcing their eye-hand coordination and understanding of spatial orientation, as well as cause and effect. One of the best possible toys is a time-tested classic: a good block set. It's just about the most open-ended, mind-expanding toy made for kids of almost all ages and one that can be used for years. Another creative, tactile-pleasing choice is modeling clay. Tambourines, xylophones, drums and other simple musical instruments are satisfying noisemakers.

Again, be sure toys are non-toxic, with no sharp edges, points or small parts that can be removed or broken off and swallowed.

3-6 years. This is the fastest growth period for the frontal lobe networks, and the speed of processing, memory, and problem-solving is increasing. The brain is at 90% of its adult weight by six years of age.

Imagination and interaction play starring roles during the preschool years, and the best toys help set the stage for developing these skills. Things that connect with kids' experiences are the best for dramatic play. Opt for a generic unstructured item rather than the single-function brand name version. Play telephones, kitchen appliances, utensils, tool sets, medical kits, dress-up clothes, and, of course, baby dolls, as well as toy people and animals, all spark scenarios kids like to construct. Finger or hand puppets offer another way of acting out and mastering day-to-day experiences.

Language and social skills practiced through make-believe games develop as preschoolers interact more frequently. Early board games introduce the concept of taking turns and sharing with others, while letter, word, and number recognition toys and games reinforce math and language learning. So, of course, do books, especially if they're chosen to match the child's interests.

Art materials (clay, crayons, markers, paints, collage materials) are another creative favorite with most children in this age group. And don't forget jump ropes, larger tricycles and that always-memorable first bike with training wheels.

6-9 years. Synaptic connections in motor and sensory areas are firmly established, and the process of elimination synapses (pruning) in these areas has begun. Because of the activity in higher brain "control" centers, children increase their levels of attention and ability to inhibit impulses.

By the time they're in the primary grades, children have gotten the hang of basic dexterity, language, and social skills; now they're eager to practice and refine them. They like to challenge themselves, intellectually, with puzzles and games that test their growing knowledge or involve strategy (checkers, card games), and physically, with pick-up sticks, jacks, roller skates, pogo sticks, and ball games.

There are lots of other imaginative options than can broaden this group's horizons, from craft sets for making jewelry and puppets to a microscope or nature-study kit. You might also turn the passion for collecting that many children develop at this age into a special link between the two of you: for example, by adding a special doll or action figure or set of stamps.

9-14 years. Maturation of the frontal lobe continues in adolescence (pruning continues during this stage). The speed and efficiency of thought increases, spatial working memory improves, emotional regulation becomes greater, planning and problem-solving skills increase, and scientific reasoning and the ability to understand one's own thinking develops. Play becomes sophisticated and increasingly symbolic.

Play in the preteen years is often a group production, and the pastimes kids prefer at this time reflect that. Many complex board games for several players and equipment for organized sports or activities (baseball bat and glove, racket/paddle games) are often a hit. Electronic games are also popular, played either on en masse or by taking competitive turns.

At the same time, preteens lavish lots of time and concentration on individual interests, which might include books, music, an elaborate construction of model-building sets, sophisticated tools, sewing kits, and paints. By this age their tastes and skills are pretty well defined, so targeting toy and entertainment purchases to the likes and abilities of each child is essential.

Supporting Play Activities

Parents can help playtime to be enjoyable, productive and safe. Here are a few suggestions on how to assist your child with play:

Provide a Child Centered Play Area:

- Make sure it is childproof and clean

- Avoid over-stimulation—especially for babies

- Allow children to leave their constructions up for a while so they come back and engage in new adventures in the world, they created

- Store play items safely but make them easily accessible

Provide Toys with Play Value That Can:

- Be used in many ways

- Allow children to determine the play

- Appeal to children at more than one age or level of development

- Be used with other toys for new and more complete play

- Stand the test of time and continue to be part of play as they develop new interests and skills

- Help children develop the skills necessary for further learning and a sense of mastery

Encourage a Balance in Play Activities:

- Reduce or eliminate screen time (1 or 2 hours per day max)

- Encourage outdoor play that uses large muscle groups–running, jumping, climbing, and playing games, for example

- Curtail time spent in adult-organized activities–kid-directed play is important

- Don't allow your child to become over-scheduled–self-directed play should be encouraged

- Encourage new activities such as art, music, building or science–you make the introduction and then let them continue the activity on their own (some will be a hit and others won't–that's okay)

- How about letting them work? Kids enjoy helping in the kitchen and in the yard–give younger children junior sized appliances, tools and equipment so they can "work" beside you

I could go on for a few more pages describing research into the benefits of play, but that would keep you from getting out of the chair and out the door with the kids. Just be sure you understand that these benefits apply to parents as well as kids. If you need more inspiration to keep your free play activities happening on a regular basis, take a look at Dr. Stuart Brown's book synthesizing his research in this fascinating area: *Play: How it Shapes the Brain, Opens the Imagination, and Invigorates the Soul.*

The Role of Parents in Play

Throughout the years that I was in full-time private practice, I saw hundreds of kids—from toddlers to teens. Often at the first visit, especially with younger children, I would end the session by saying to the parents, "My first prescription is very helpful but often what I hear from parents is that it is not as easy to follow as one might think." The typical response from the parent was, "Oh, I will do anything you say. Don't worry."

When I told them that what I wanted them to do was to find about 15 to 20 minutes each day to do something fun with their child, I often heard, "Oh, you know, when I come home, I'm tired from a tough day at work and I have so many things to do so it's really hard to do that."

I would then say, "Please give it a try and you'll be surprised how it will change the relationship between you and your child. And guess what? I can't think of a better way to relieve some of that stress than for you to connect with your inner child and have some fun." Sometimes it took a session or two to get them to try it, but most finally did. They were amazed at how it was often the key to turning things around. For many, it became something they looked forward to on their way home.

Of course, as children move on developmentally from baby to toddler, and eventually on to a teenager, their preferences change. But in healthy kids, their desire to spend time with their parent(s) continues. When a healthy parent-child relationship exists, the desire to play with their parents continues as well.

Playing with your child continuously through the years develops a strong bond built from love and respect that can be drawn upon during tense moments and tough times. Play is also essential for learning, and playfulness can help one cope with difficult issues when they come up.

Playing with Your Child

While children do need time to play alone and with other children without adult intervention, research shows that playtime with parents is also critical.

Children crave quality time with parents. It makes them feel special. Parents are encouraged to find time to spend playing with their kids on a regular basis. This should include one on one time with each child and group time with all of the adults and kids in the home. If you're a single parent or have an only child, occasionally invite family or friends over to play.

In pretend play, let your child develop the theme. Get into their world. Let them go with it. Ask questions. Play along. Be silly along with them and have fun. Avoid over-stimulation and know when it is time to stop.

Also, when appropriate, parents can use stuffed animals or puppets to act out real-life situations that can teach problem solving or social skills. Let the puppet demonstrate the wrong way to handle a situation. Then, along with input from your child, act out a better way. Afterward, let your child do the same.

More Possibilities:

- Play outdoors. Throw balls. Push kids on swings. Make mud pies. Go on a hike around the neighborhood. Take a nature walk in your backyard.

- Play games–card games–board games–silly and wacky kid's games. Help them learn to take turns, how to win and how to lose. Praise them. Encourage them. Laugh with them.

- Get involved in a craft project together. Build a jigsaw puzzle as a family. Bake cookies. Paint a picture.

- Listen to music together. Sing along. Play rhythm instruments along with music. Get out the guitar or keyboard and make music.

- Read a book together. Ask questions. Ask them to change the story or make up a new one.

- Watch a movie together. Find out what they liked and how they felt. Discover your child's interests. Comment on and discuss any bothersome content, whether that is words or actions.

- Play kid games such as: Follow the Leader–Guess What I Am? –Hide and Seek

- Help kids when they show the need it or ask for it. Use it as a time to teach:

  - patience

  - problem solving

  - social skills

  - creativity

Playing and spending time with kids builds a bond that will last forever. It lets the child know he or she is loved and appreciated. It opens the door for sharing problems and concerns when the need arises. It helps the parent get to know and understand the uniqueness of each child. It's also an excellent stress reducer for overworked parents.

Family activities are great for the whole family. They help develop strong family bonds which can last a lifetime. You may have heard the saying, "a family who plays together stays together." Such families are also more cooperative, supportive and have open communication. These qualities pay off in big dividends by increasing self-esteem, social skills and a sense of connectedness that helps kids and teens use good judgment when confronted with difficulties and temptations.

Family Game Night. Here's a great tradition that's easy to start. Pick a night and make it a family game night. Gradually add games that can be fun for the entire family. Take turns choosing the game to play (make sure the games are appropriate for the youngest player). This is a great time to bond through friendly competition. Children learn how to take turns and play fair. They also learn how to be a good loser and well as a good winner.

Encourage Outdoor Activities. Now is the time to stop the "Couch Potato" syndrome. Pediatricians find that most kids are not getting enough exercise. Parents can be good role models by going outside and playing along with their kids. Hey, it's good for adults as well. Encourage your child to be active. Help them to develop motor coordination and learn good sportsmanship.

It's All About Family Fun

Food? Shelter? Eating a vegetable with every meal? Health insurance? You might think of these as the basics—the essential ingredients of a healthy childhood in a nurturing family. But if you look closely at the list, one of the essentials is missing: family fun. Why does fun deserve to be on the same list as food and shelter? Research by psychologist Dr. Peter Gray, published in the *American Journal of Play*, suggests that play is an essential adaptive survival activity in groups, and has been since the days of early humankind. Free play, he says, is particularly important to children, and there are indications that this type of play has dwindled in most children's lives.

Free play is game or imaginative activity that is freely chosen, age-mixed, and minimally competitive. It's the kind of play that arises spontaneously when kids gather. Think of it as the, "Here we are in the vacant lot with nothing but a piece of string and five bottle caps, so what do we do now?" kind of play. Adult-organized activities such as soccer games or kit-building projects aren't bad, they just don't include free play and aren't the kind of fun that gives children the most benefit.

You may have let family fun slip off the list because your family budget is looking worse than the national budget, or because stress and time have given you a case of "fun amnesia." If that's the case, then you've noticed that dull haze that develops during the day, and those instances where you realize you can't remember the last time you laughed out loud. If this is the case in your household, it's time to inject fun back into your family's environment. But where to start? Try to remember the joy you found during free play when you were growing up. Did it involve digging action figure-sized tunnels in a vacant lot and filling them with water? Was there a craze that played itself out with the kids in the neighborhood, like a loosely organized kickball tournament? When you were younger, you may recall playing make-believe by dressing up or at least acting like a favorite TV or movie character or molding with play dough. Are you getting the picture?

The best ingredients for free play fun involve an attitude of curiosity, some room to explore and a measure of freedom from adult direction. This is what Stuart Brown and other researchers have found sets the stage for mind-healthy play. You may also notice that this type of activity builds on itself organically and doesn't require progression toward an end goal.

Achievement, if present in the activity, is part of the play and not a means to an end. Why does this kind of play tend to occur outdoors? It may be due to having fewer restrictions outside of the house.

If you're having a hard time coming up with ideas to initiate family play, try some of these fun-starters. Just be mindful that once the kids are involved, managing their choices during this time needs to be avoided:

- Set up some toys or action figures around a tree or in strategic places in the yard and ask your kids to show you what the characters would do if they came to life.

- Make a boat out of paper and tape, put some water in the tub, and ask if the kids can make one.

- Bring out a ball and make a "rule" about what each person has to do with the ball while walking across the yard.

- Snow day? Have a "migloo" building contest, that is, a miniature igloo building contest.

- Make snow angels but finish them off by making some pans of colored water with food coloring and "paint" the wings of the angels.

- Make or buy a playhouse for outdoors.

- Put a blanket over a card table to make a tent, a house, a cave or a fort. You can play with them and you can let them play on their own.

In addition to spending time in free and imaginative play, the use of other toys and games can produce hours of fun and learning as well.

On a family fun night, you can play card games, board games or interactive games, such as *Simon* or *Hungry, Hungry Hippos*. These are great fun, and some help develop problem-solving abilities, memory, language skills, coordination, and social skills.

Science kits of all kinds stimulate curiosity and discovery learning. You can do experiments along with your child as well as encourage them to work on their own or with other children.

Building toys such as blocks, or Legos can provide hours of interactive fun. You can build anything you can imagine–this is an opportunity to encourage creativity and free play. You can help your kids with fine motor skills as well as model and teach patience and persistence with these activities. You can also bring in toys such as cars, trucks, or action figures and add more imagination and fantasy play to the mix.

By now, hopefully, you're getting the picture that once children are permitted to use their imaginations and trust that they have the freedom to do so; they will come up with some great ideas on their own.

Lakeshore is a teacher supply store that now has an online presence. This is a wonderful website for parents to find all kinds of creative play materials that you probably won't find in toy stores or at traditional online sources for toys. My wife was an elementary school teacher, and she would visit our local Lakeshore store to buy materials and supplies for her classroom. When our children were young, she also found amazing toys, educational materials, and creative playthings for them. One I always remember was a tunnel that was made by attaching cloth to a large metal coil. It could be crunched for storage, but our children would spend hours playing with it, connecting the tunnel from a table to a tent to a large closet, which they called their "secret fort." I highly recommend a visit to discover excellent resources for your young children. [lakeshorelearning.com]

CHAPTER 6
Family Traditions and Family Activities

WHEN I HEAR THE words "family traditions," the first thoughts that come to mind are centered on the holidays. For me, that's Christmas. I remember the annual traditions from my childhood days, as well as those we established in our family home. While traditions do tend to change somewhat as children grow older, they continue to bring back fond memories for years to come. Traditions are something we look forward to, and they must be done the same way each year—unless there is agreement from everyone for making changes, of course.

Societies through the ages have established traditions to celebrate the changing of the seasons, to celebrate the passages of life (birthdays, weddings, etc.,) and to commemorate specific occasions, such as historical events. The repeated rituals we conduct for each particular celebration provides a sense of stability and comfort. There may be special meals, decorations or activities that are reproduced as close as possible to past occasions. There's the star that goes on the top of the Christmas tree, Aunt Susie's cookies, a trip to the lake, or listening to certain music, to name a few. One of the best parts of traditions is they give us something to look forward to and anticipate. We can count on them—they bring a sense of order and peace to a chaotic and stressful world.

While these types of traditions are beautiful experiences, they are infrequent. Families can build on this aspect of human nature by establishing their own routines, which could be daily, weekly, monthly, or seasonally. Family activities of all kinds are significant in that they encourage connectedness, communication, and sharing in fun, meaningful experiences.

When family members agree to engage in regularly scheduled activities together, they become something to expect and anticipate. Each family member can provide suggestions for how to conduct the events. Family traditions should be agreed to by all family members, and they should be held sacred. This means that once agreed upon, all family members commit to making that time available and work their schedules around these family events as much as possible. Usually, that isn't a problem, and you'll find your children will remind you when the time is getting close.

Here are some ideas for weekly or monthly activities you can establish as family traditions:

Family Game Night. Pick a day either weekly, biweekly or monthly when you set aside a specific time to play a game together. These can be simple card games, board games, or occasionally even video games, such as *Wii Sports Resort* (one of my favorites). Playing games allows everyone to engage in friendly competition and most of all, laugh together. They also provide teaching moments for social skills such as sharing, being a good winner as well as a good loser, and complimenting and encouraging others, to name a few.

Family Movie Night. Select a day, a time, cue up a family-friendly flick on Netflix, break out the popcorn, and enjoy. Have a few laughs or become engrossed in a drama or mystery. When appropriate, you can spend time discussing the plot of the movie as well as individual thoughts and feelings about the characters or storyline.

Family Recreational Outing. This is a great way to have fun while getting out of the house and engaging in physical activity or sharing an event. Bowling, miniature golf, swimming, hiking, walking in the park, skating, bike riding, and skiing are a few suggestions for physical activities you can try together.

Attending a sporting event, movie, play or concert as a family is also lots of fun. Try to include a family meal before or after the activity as an additional way to use this time to connect.

Educational Outing. You can have a great time as a family going to the local library, a museum, or taking a nature walk. How about signing up for art or music lessons together? Again, don't feel like you need to always go as an entire family each time. Maybe you have one child who is more of a book-worm, and another who loves exploring the woods. As parents, it's okay to divide your time so you can be with your children separately while enjoying their passions.

Reading and Singing Aloud. This promotes feelings of closeness and instills an appreciation for books and music. Encourage your children to suggest books and music and introduce them to new experiences as well. Share one of your favorite books you read as a child or some of your favorite music. After reading together, discuss the book, including what thoughts and feelings it elicited in your child. Go online together to learn more about a subject, author or musical artist that particularly interests him or her.

Share a Hobby. Again, this may be an activity for the entire family or smaller family units, depending on the activity and age. You could set out a puzzle and let family members work on it in their spare time, either individually or as a pair. Arts and crafts projects can be fun to work on together, as well as model building, scrapbooking and gardening. With younger children, these types of projects can help with developing fine motor skills, as well as patience and frustration tolerance.

Family Vacations. Traveling together as a family can be a wonderful tradition. Road trips, camping, visits to the beach or mountains, or visiting a new state or country are fantastic opportunities for bonding and having fun together as a family. If you can make family vacations an annual event, it can become something that the whole family not only looks forward to with excitement and anticipation each year but also looks back on fondly years later.

Spiritual Activities. For those families who are religious, attending services, engaging in regular spiritual practices such as prayer or being active in your spiritual community are lovely ways to connect and share common values and experiences. Even families that aren't necessarily religious often enjoy creating their own spiritual activities that they engage in regularly.

As I mentioned earlier, life gets hectic. The daily routine can wear down anyone, and sometimes the hours disappear before you realize it. If you find your family in a pinch for time, try to carve out just 20 minutes to be together and do something active. Take a family bike ride, slap on hockey skates and hit the pond, or go for a walk with the family dog. Just a little bit of time spent doing something active together gives everyone a chance to refocus on the most important people in their lives: each other.

In truth, there's never a bad time to work on building and strengthening the bond between parents and children, as well as between siblings. The problem many families face is a lack of options. Without good ideas, most families end up spending time together in the same room, but Dad is watching TV while the kids play on smartphones and tablets, and Mom reads a magazine. The key to family bonding is putting aside the distractions and spending quality time together, no matter what you're doing. For now, I'd like you to start thinking about ideas for activities your family could start engaging in on regularly.

Here are a few suggestions to get you started:

- A weekend getaway is a short, simple way to break out of the routine and get a chance to spend some quality time together as a family without the distractions of everyday life. The best part is this idea applies all-year round! Rent a cabin in the woods during the winter, hit the beach in the summer, or break out the tents in the fall. There's no wrong way to spend a weekend with family.

- Completing a project together is a great way to improve teamwork within the family. Everyone has a role to play when tackling a household project and everyone can share in the sense of pride that comes from caring for the home that you all share. This can be as simple as getting some fresh air together while raking leaves, or if you have older kids, you could try tackling a minor renovation in your home. Whatever you do, give everyone a role and reward the family as a group for completing the project.

• Every city in America offers residents a chance to come together, get to know one another, and even do some good for their neighbors through community events. Whether you attend a social outing or give your time at a charitable event hosted by your city, joining a community event as a family is a great way to spend time together. It helps build a family bond that includes a sense of togetherness with those people who inhabit your local area.

Work, school, extracurricular activities, screen time, and daily routine tasks pull families in all different directions. Trying to come together can often feel like herding cats. Organizing schedules should be intentional, requiring the cooperation and commitment of all family members. Here are a few suggestions to help your family's plans come together more successfully:

Family Meetings. It's good to plan some time on certain days of the week when the entire family can come together and share what's happening in their lives. For example, you can ask each family member to talk about what has been the best and worst part of their week. Setting this special time aside not only brings families closer together but becomes a safe haven for your kids to come to with their concerns. In Chapter 16, we will focus more in-depth on planning and holding regular family meetings.

Family Calendar. Have one large calendar that everyone can use to add all of their after-school programs, work meetings, etc. This way everyone knows what each family member is up to, which can also make planning family time easier. Seeing the types of activities each person is involved with can open up the line of communication at family meetings. For example, a parent or sibling can ask how a particular child's soccer match was, or if they're enjoying tutoring. This is a great way to help kids and parents show interest in each other and to be more inclusive.

Remember, a family that plays together, stays together, and becomes the gift that keeps on giving lovingly for a lifetime.

CHAPTER 7
Connecting with Your Kids

AT ONE POINT OR another, all parents fear that they aren't connecting with their children as effectively as they would like. You might start to worry that you don't know them as well as you should, or that they may be doing things that you would not approve. The fear can be almost paralyzing. The good news is that this problem can be solved, and it isn't difficult. By even desiring to connect with the children in your life, you're already making great strides toward your goal. It's important to care about them and what goes on around them. Take time to realize that you're doing a good thing, and that should help boost your confidence on the matter.

For most parents, the desire to love and provide for their child is as natural as breathing. But the truth is, today people are constantly inundated with text messages, social media, non-traditional work schedules, hundreds of channels on television, and increased financial demands. As a result, more parents than ever are struggling to feel genuinely connected to their child.

It's normal to become slightly removed in your involvement as your child becomes more independent, but children still need to know they have someone to turn to whenever life becomes challenging.

Here are a few tactics to help you become a more connected parent:

The Special 20

As I mentioned earlier, one of the most important things a parent can do is to spend 15 to 20 minutes of quality time with each of their children, either individually or as a group, as many days of the week as possible. I also put this into practice with my own children when they were growing up. In a way, you can look at this as another routine, but it's you committing to personally connect with each of your children daily.

For parents, making this commitment is not always easy, and I understand that. When we reflect on the hurried schedule of the typical family, it doesn't seem possible. You're already spending time taking your kids to activities, helping with homework, getting them ready for bed, and countless other tasks. However, these activities don't provide the unstructured time for just having fun. The *Special 20* can be the magical touch that brings about a significant change in the parent-child relationship.

Spending this time together will improve cooperation. It reduces sibling rivalry because your child is receiving unconditional, individual attention. By unconditional, I mean it's not earned by doing chores or completing homework, and it should happen even on a day when there may have been a significant problem, such as getting into trouble at school or having an argument at home. Appropriately addressing those incidents is important, but the *Special 20* time should still occur sometime before the end of the day.

There are many activities you can engage in during *Special 20* time. Let your child suggest some things he or she would like to do. With younger children, child-directed playtime might be the way to go. Playing games, reading, and building with LEGOs or blocks can all be fun activities for younger children. I have provided a table at the end of this chapter with more suggestions you could use to get the process started. Once you have faithfully implemented this for three to four weeks, you won't need a chart. Playtime will become a natural part of your life, and one that both you and your child will look forward to and enjoy.

Additional Ways Parents Can Connect with Children

Talk (and Listen) to Them. The simplest way to connect with your children is to talk to them. Tell them about your day and ask about theirs. Try to remember everything they tell you. Children have a memory that just won't quit sometimes, and they expect you to have the same. It's essential for your child to feel like you care about what they have to say. Ask questions about what they told you to prove you were listening and want to know more. Don't expect your kids to tell you everything about themselves in one sitting. It takes time to build the kind of connection you're looking for, especially with teens and older children who will from time-to-time naturally feel the need for more independence which they interpret to be maintaining some distance.

Take an Interest in Their Interests. Just talking doesn't work for all kids. They may have built their guard up too high to realize that you want to join them in some of their activities. In this case, it may be a good idea to consider doing something else together. If your child enjoys playing video games, ask for the second controller and join in. Maybe help them with an art project. You can try to get involved in anything they like to do. They may still try to shut you out at times, but eventually, you'll find something to do together. Just try not to seem judgmental about their hobbies. If they start to feel that you don't appreciate what they love, they will begin to push you further away.

Invite Your Kids into Your World. If you can't find common ground in the things they like to do, you might want to take a look for some in the things you enjoy. It's not uncommon for children to forget that parents or guardians are people too. If you're willing to show them who you are, then perhaps they will open up and do the same. You can invite them to watch one of your favorite shows or sporting events. Let them meet some of your co-workers. If your children are old enough, you can take them with you to the gym or your yoga class. Anything can work if you can get them interested.

Take Your Child along When You Are Out Running Errands. This is easy to do. If you have more than one child, have them take turns going with you. You'll be surprised what might come up in a casual conversation on one of these trips. Children sometimes feel more comfortable to open up when they are one-on-one with just one parent in the car. You can also teach them how to get around town, how to shop, how to budget money, and much more.

Find a New Hobby. You may find that you have no current interests in common with your child–that's okay. In this case, you can talk to them about finding something new for the two of you to do together. Try to find something that neither of you have done, and you both find at least mildly interesting to start together. Neither of you will be the leader in this activity because no one has more experience. Even if you find out that you both disliked it, you at least shared a mutual experience.

Don't Get Discouraged. Establishing a solid parent-child connection can be difficult. It may seem that no matter what you try, you're still feeling just as distant from your children as when you started. Don't give up. They will know what you're trying to do, and on some level, they appreciate it, even if they don't make it obvious right from the start. If nothing else, they will at least think of you when they face any struggles and remember that at least one person cares for them–sometimes that's enough.

Suggestions for Connecting with Teens

Do you ever feel as if your teenager is from another planet–that they speak a language you don't understand? Or that they have interests you've never heard of? It's a common phenomenon.

Teenagers at times can be challenging to engage in meaningful conversation. Some go through a stage where they feel it isn't cool to spend time with a parent. That said, they're *your* teenagers, and there are steps you can take to understand them better and be closer.

In later chapters, I'll cover several ways to connect with kids of all ages, including family mealtimes, fitness, and reading. The earlier chapter on family traditions and activities also provides more ideas for activities you can do with your teen that will help you to connect. Below are a few more suggestions to consider. It's not uncommon for teens to feel more comfortable with the same-gender parent, but there are times when either parent may have a unique interest or ability that only they can share regardless of gender. If you have teens that are close in age, you could make it a family activity.

Ask Questions and Listen. The first step to understanding your teen is to ask questions but be strategic about it. Many teens give "yes" or "no" answers when you ask them a question. The trick is to engage them when they're more likely to open up, such as when they aren't with friends or running around. Driving in the car seems to be a good time, assuming they don't have headphones on.

When you ask questions, make sure to listen to the answers. If you don't understand half of the words they're using, it's okay to ask for clarification. As you're listening, take mental notes—this will also come in handy for the next step below.

Google It! If you have no idea what your child is talking about, look it up. Google the things and people they express interest in, and even the language they use. *Urban Dictionary* [urbandictionary.com] can also be incredibly useful.

Get Involved. Start taking an active interest in your older child or teen's interests. Volunteer at local organizations, or at activities that they're involved with, such as sports or scouts. Keep up with the things that they post and share on social media.

Play Hooky. If weekends aren't an option, then consider a weekday. This isn't an activity you can repeat often, but once or twice a year you might skip work and take your teen out of school. Spend the day together. Go to lunch. Take your child to see a matinee movie, head to the beach or go shopping. It could also be playing a round of golf, taking a hike in the woods, or playing video games at an "old school" arcade. Teenagers enjoy and appreciate traditions. You and your teen can make your day an annual event.

Take a Day Trip. As I mentioned earlier, teenagers tend to open up in the car. It's amazing the conversations that you can have with your son or daughter while driving. Plan a day trip, just the two of you, and head out for an adventure. You might drive somewhere for a hike, or head to a nearby city to play tourists. Visit galleries and museums, go shopping or attend a festival.

Volunteer Together. Find a cause that is near and dear to your teen and donate your time. Check out the local animal shelter, hospital, nursing home, and other charities to find something you can both get behind. It could be a walk or run to raise funds for a worthy cause, participating in a beach clean-up, serving meals at a soup kitchen, or spending time with children at a youth shelter.

Get Creative. Find hobbies you can share, such as blogging, woodworking, crafts, photography or music. Attend events related to specific interest, like concerts or art museums.

Relax. Each generation has their own trends, language, and interests. When you were a teenager, your parents thought you were from another planet as well. It comes with the territory. It's normal and okay not to be able to relate with your teenager completely. Do what you can to connect with them. Let them know that you're interested in their lives– and then relax. You don't need to be best friends with your teenager, nor do you need to share the same interests. It's enough just to let them know that you care about what they're up to and you'll always be there for them.

CHAPTER 8

Personal Space

How to Connect with Your Child without Overdoing It

ALL PARENTS WANT TO connect and be involved with their children. Children of involved parents feel more confident, assured, and have a higher level of self-esteem. They tend to excel in school and do well in extracurricular activities as well as with their hobbies. But is there such a thing as too much involvement? In a word–yes. It's imperative when you're becoming involved with your school-aged child's activities and academics that you recognize the distinction between being an involved parent and a parent that is overly involved.

It's crucial that you don't intrude too much into your child's privacy. Children need their space to develop their skills, talents, and abilities. In our eagerness to help our children succeed, it's tempting to want to step in and start doing things for them if they're doing it incorrectly or inadequately. But remember– you had to learn, too, and this is their chance to learn on their own.

Be there to encourage and support your child and offer praise at a job well done. But also, remember to step back and allow your child to learn from their own mistakes and to develop their own way of doing things. There's usually more than one way to do something and just because your child is doing it differently than you would doesn't make it wrong. Who knows? You might learn a little something from your child, as well.

Finally, encourage your child to share their troubles with you so that you can help them sort through their problems. If they say they don't want to talk about it or need some time to figure things out for themselves, respect that by letting them know you're available whenever they need you. Allowing your child to figure out how to deal with their problems—with you there for support—is an integral part of growing up.

When to Leave Your Teen Alone

Raising teenagers can be a terrifying experience. Often there are no easy answers, and every parent has a different struggle with their teen. However, every teen is going through the same changes. This is the time when they begin their transition into adulthood. They're striving to discover who they are, independently of their families, and who they want to be. As this happens, teens look for more space to work through the changes—they need to dissociate from their parents to do this.

While it's difficult for parents to leave their teen alone, it can sometimes be necessary. For a parent to watch their child struggle is one of the hardest experiences they can face, but teens need to work things out for themselves. They have had their parents holding their hands throughout their childhood, but eventually, they need to learn to be their own person.

There are times when it isn't appropriate to give a teenager space. Parents need to maintain boundaries for safe behaviors. Teens still need guidance, proof that their parents care, and are looking out for them. Teens often have a sense of indestructibility that can lead to risky behaviors, especially with the Internet as a tool.

Parents shouldn't give their teenagers unlimited privacy and trust if they haven't earned them. Parents need to base their decisions about boundaries on their teen's current and past behavior. They need to know that their actions are affecting their parents and that if they've abused trust in the past, this is the reason they aren't able to have certain privileges.

Teens need to make some decisions that have an impact on their lives. Parents should encourage their independence with summer or school-year jobs and hold teenagers accountable for their performance. Teens can also benefit from being left alone with their own financial decisions. Parents can give advice but shouldn't be overbearing about it. Instead, they should let teens come to their own conclusions. But this also means letting them deal with the consequences of their decisions, even if those consequences are negative. As part of the growing up experience, teens shouldn't be shielded from their mistakes as this is necessary for their development and eventual independence.

When a teen asks for space, they should have it when appropriate. As a maturing adolescent, their bond and relationship with their parents needs to mature as well. In that awkward, transitioning age, teens need boundaries and their own space. Parents find it difficult to walk this fine line and often find ourselves coming down too hard on one side or the other. Mistakes happen, and parenting will never be perfect. It's important for parents to try to remember that their emerging adult won't always have them there, and now is the time they need a safe space with their parents close by in which to discover who they will be.

Some Ways to Make Your Marriage or Relationship a Priority

Children are wonderful. They also make it a little challenging to find time for yourself and your marriage. When you make your marriage (or relationship, or individual time) a priority, you not only enjoy the benefits, but your family and children also thrive. It's important to take steps to find quality time with your partner. The following tips and ideas will help you and your spouse. If you're a single parent, you still need time away with your friends or to engage in group activities through an organization you belong to, such as a book club, church, sports team, or going to a gym.

Create Small Rituals. Date night is something that people often recommend to married couples with children. However, it usually doesn't work. It can be difficult and expensive to find a reliable babysitter. Designating a specific night as "date night" can put some stress on the evening. Instead, consider creating small rituals that connect you each day. For example, spend five minutes each morning drinking coffee together and talking about your day. Go to bed at the same time and spend time together. Turn off your devices and snuggle, talk, and enjoy intimacy. Text each other every day at lunch or connect at the end of the workday as you're heading home. Small rituals can make a significant difference in your marriage and your life. Stay connected.

Support Each Other's Interests. Find something outside of work and children that you enjoy doing and support each other to pursue those interests, either together or individually. For example, you might want to take tennis lessons, and your husband likes to golf. Take turns. He takes tennis lessons with you, and you go golfing with him. This gets you active and engaged with each other outside of work and family. It helps you connect on a deeper level and appreciate each other.

Practice Gratitude. It's easy to focus on the negative things, such as the things your spouse does that get on your nerves or the tasks he or she doesn't do around the home. Let the negative emotions go and focus on what you love and enjoy about each other. Is your partner funny, kind, or intelligent? What talents and virtues does he or she have that you appreciate? Don't just think about why you love your spouse but tell them—and tell them often. Focusing on the positive and expressing it to your spouse powerfully connects you. It's important to know you're appreciated and loved.

Spend Time Together. Enjoy walks, holding hands, and doing the things that make you feel connected. Watch a TV show or movie together. Making your marriage a priority isn't as tricky as it sounds. Communicate and connect throughout the day if possible. This is not only positive for your children to see, but it's also essential for a happy and healthy marriage.

CHAPTER 9
Family Reading Time

IN A RECENT SURVEY, one in three parents said they read bedtime stories with their children every night. However, over half of the parents reported that their kids spend more time with video games and television than with books, and an alarming percentage of families do not have any books in their home at all. Encouraging your children and teens to read books is vital to their academic achievement. A study comparing time spent reading books versus the use of digital devices (such as computers, smartphones, tablets and television) among a group of USA children ages eight to twelve published in the April 2018 edition of *Acta Pediatrica* concluded that time spent reading had a positive effect on the development of language, executive functions, and academic performance, while screen time had a negative effect.

Today, kids go to the computer to look up information, and many parents and teachers believe that watching videos and interacting with computer-based learning programs are just as good as or better than reading books. However, research in the USA and other countries continues to find that reading books is far superior to various forms of digital information systems. Reading aloud has also been found to improve memory of material.

In a policy statement on literacy promotion published by the American Academy of Pediatrics in 2014, the introduction states, "Reading regularly with young children stimulates optimal patterns of brain development and strengthens parent-child relationships at a critical time in child development, which, in turn, builds language, literacy, and social-emotional skills that last a lifetime."

This means reading to your kids is not just a pleasant thing to do–it's critical to their development. They will be better prepared to start school, and once they're in school, a calm evening ritual helps get kids ready to sleep. After the usual chaos of the day, which often includes television shows or video games that can wind a child up, spending 10-15 minutes simply being still and listening to a story helps your child calm down. Focusing on a restful activity slows his mind down and his body relaxes at the same time. Parents often find this habit has the same calming effect on them. Time spent this way divides the active part of the day from the night's rest, and helps your child make that transition.

Looking at a book while someone reads helps kids get ready to start reading themselves. Think about everything a child is taking in when looking at a book, even before they know how to read. She's learning what letters look like, and that words are composed of groups of letters. She sees that pages are read from left to right and top to bottom–basic stuff, but no one knows it automatically! These basics need to be learned before one can even attempt to read. Also, reading helps your child learn new vocabulary words and some of the differences between spoken and written language.

Reading helps build a child's imagination. When a child views a television show, the story is all there for him. He watches and takes it in without having to engage his brain. When reading a book, or having a book read to him, however, he must bring his own effort to the process. He should have a picture in his head of what is happening, creating the experience in his mind. Children who enjoy being read to also enjoy looking at books on their own and using their memory to retell the story to themselves.

Reading helps children learn about their world. Children's books, especially picture books, often reinforce the familiar events of a child's life: going to bed, going to school, habits of hygiene and nutrition, etc. Seeing characters in a book take baths, brush teeth, and say goodnight to toys gives a context for her own daily routine. Other books can teach your child about things she has not yet encountered, such as going to a new school, visiting a zoo or a museum, or traveling on an airplane.

Reading with your children strengthens your bond with them. Bedtime reading means that the last event in your child's day is a few moments of peaceful, calm time with mom or dad. If a book raises questions for your child, he can ask them. A story can also give you a chance to talk with your child about a concern you have. Most of all, it builds an emotional connection and allows an opportunity to end the day with some parental affection and cuddle time.

With advances in technology, reading is becoming a lost art as kids are increasingly finding other activities in which to engage. However, it's important to remember that reading is truly fundamental. Children, who develop a love of reading, develop a love for learning. Reading texts and instructions requires more than a rudimentary understanding of the English language. Even kids who don't attend college need to have skills and vocabulary that can be learned by constant reading. So, how can you make sure your kids read? Here are a few tips:

Set a Good Example. When parents have books around and read on a regular basis, kids see it as a worthwhile activity. Even if you read magazines, practice what you preach to gain their interest.

Offer a Variety of Materials They Like. Reading the classics is a great ambition, but many teens are not interested in them–at least not yet. Ask them what type of subjects they would like to read about and get it for them. It can be magazines, graphic novels, or vampire teen romance novels. Suspend your judgment of the subject matter in favor of getting your children to read. Just use your common sense if you think the material might be inappropriate.

Find Books That Focus on Their Interests. Talk to your child about what interests them. Point them to books and magazines that relate to their interests—it could be books about dinosaurs, astronomy, or a particular sport. Kids enjoy books that stir their imagination, make them laugh, and have characters that are like them in some way. Find out what characters they like most from movies or TV shows.

Get Your Child a Library Card. Take your child to the public library and get them a card. Introduce him or her to the children's librarian. Find out what activities the library might offer for children on the weekends and during vacation time.

Use Technology. Kids like to carry as few things as possible. But, if they have an iPod or a smartphone, you're in luck. Audiobooks are downloadable, so your child can listen to their books on the go. Or offer to get them an eBook reader. That way they can store all their books in one place, and easily take them along wherever they go. The Kindle and Nook also offer applications for smartphones, so your child can read books or magazines whenever they want. You can choose to exclude reading time from screen time limits. This is different from screen time—for some, it's a more convenient way of reading books. It's not watching videos or reading brief articles on the Internet of dubious accuracy and quality.

Choose a Specific Time for Reading. Choose a specific time for reading. Most teens use their peak hours to hang out with friends or do other activities. Decide on a time when they don't have anything going on. It can be "family time," and everyone can spend time reading.

Let Your Child or Teen Read to You. Sharing their interests lets them know you care. Encouraging them to read a comic, a passage from their favorite book, newspaper, or magazine to you beefs up their reading skills and can foster great discussions.

Here Are a Few Hints for Reading to and with Children:

1. Try to use inflections to indicate action and imitate separate characters to draw kids into the story.

2. Use a sense of humor when appropriate.

3. Share your take on the book. Discuss interesting details and information in the story.

4. Get your child's perspective on the book.

5. Make up a story together or have them make up their own story.

6. With older children, you can take turns reading parts of the story.

7. Have your child draw a picture related to the book.

8. You can help with vocabulary building by looking up new words. For more tips on how to read to children, I highly recommend *The Read Aloud Handbook* by Jim Trelease.

Section 1 – Connectedness - Summary

Ideas & Recommendations for Increasing Connectedness in Your Family

Suggested First Steps to Improving Connectedness in Your Family:

1. Develop your parenting mission statement and parenting plan.

2. Practice mindfulness daily.

3. Look for times when you can join your kids in play.

4. Start using the *Special 20* approach with each child. Use the Special Time Worksheet to get started. In time, it will become a regular part of your life that you and your kids will look forward to and enjoy.

5. Start holding your family meetings (See Chapter 16 for suggestions).

6. During your family meeting, start to plan and schedule family activities. The Game Night and Movie Night charts may help.

7. Make reading time part of your *Special 20* activities (at least once per week).

8. In your family meeting, consider starting a Family Reading Challenge. Set a beginning and ending date. Set reasonable goals based on the age and ability of each participant (that means parents too). Plan a group celebration at the conclusion of the challenge. No need for individual rewards, just celebrate the group effort.

Tools for Success: Connectedness

Family Game Night. Use this simple chart during family meetings to jot down ideas for games and meals or snacks. You can then plan ahead and have everything you need.

- Try to make this a regular event on the same day and time. Frequency could be weekly, twice a month, or monthly depending on time and interest.

- This is an excellent time to work on team building, communication, and sportsmanship. Some kids need help learning to take turns, appropriately handling winning or losing, and coping with frustration.

Movie Night. Like above, this helps with planning and getting input from everyone on what to watch.

- Again, try to have a regular schedule.

- This is a great time to work on communication and comprehension. Ask questions about what family members liked best, how they would rate the movie, discuss historical, geographical or biographical information when applicable (look things up online), and discuss how problems were resolved. "Who was your favorite character? Why did you like them? Do they remind you of anyone you know? Did any character annoy you? Why?" etc.

- Use the movie as a time to encourage reading. If the movie was based on a book, suggest reading it and comparing the book to the film. If it was about a historical figure or event, suggest reading more on the subject.

Special Time. This worksheet helps in selecting activities you can do during special time and to commit to a time. Using this tool will increase the likelihood that you'll be able to initiate and continue this important connectedness component. If you stick with it, it will become a routine that both you and your kids will look forward to participating in.

My Reading Log. This worksheet will keep track of each kids reading activity but also encourage understanding and appreciation of the reading material. Each time you initial, you can offer praise and encouragement as well as engage in a discussion about the material covered. Questions such as those suggested for Movie Night help to improve reading comprehension skills.

Please be sure to visit parentingtoday.com/tools for PDF versions of the charts provided at the end of each section as well as additional resources, including updates, classes, and forums for parents.

Family Game Night

Our Favorite Games	Meal Ideas
Games We Want to Try	Snack Ideas

Movie Night

Schedule for This Month

Day, Date & Time	Movie	Snacks

Ideas for Future Movie Nights

Movie Ideas	Snack Ideas

Special Time Suggested Activities & Schedule

Arts and Crafts	o Make holiday decorations o Glue sticks together o Build and pint models o Build and paint birdhouses	o Paper bag/paper plate masks o Nature mobiles o Photo collages o String beads
Bake and Cook	o Bake goods from a mix o Make parts of dinner o Make pancakes o Make cookie-cutter cookies	
Sports Activities	o Play catch o Go for a hike o Bike riding o Play HORSE (basketball)	o Flag football o Skate boarding/roller blading Scooter ride
Out for Food	o Breakfast diner-type place o Fast food with playland o Ice cream, frozen yogurt	
Story Time	o Read to your child o Play instruments	
Play Games	o SORRY! o Twister o Clue o Boggle	o Card games (go fish, war) Hide and seek o Tag
Build Things	o Legos o K'nex o Lincoln Logs	
Imaginative Play	o Puppets o Charades	
Out and About	o Garden o Picnic o Park o Age-appropriate museum	o Zoo o Pet store, reptile/fish store

Other Ideas: _____

_____

Schedule some time and make a commitment.

Week 1	Monday	Tuesday	Wednesday	Thursday	Friday	Saturday	Sunday
Time							
Activity							

Week 2	Monday	Tuesday	Wednesday	Thursday	Friday	Saturday	Sunday
Time							
Activity							

My Reading Log

Name: _____

Date	Book	Pages	Initials

☐ What I Liked Best or ☐ What I Learned:

☐ What I Liked Best or ☐ What I Learned:

☐ What I Liked Best or ☐ What I Learned:

☐ What I Liked Best or ☐ What I Learned:

☐ What I Liked Best or ☐ What I Learned:

☐ What I Liked Best or ☐ What I Learned:

☐ What I Liked Best or ☐ What I Learned:

☐ What I Liked Best or ☐ What I Learned:

SECTION 2 –
Open Communication

Open communication results in each family member feeling loved and respected. It also makes it easier to handle conflicts when they arise. The basics include listening, empathy, supportive communication, and collaborative problem-solving to resolve conflicts.

Chapter 10: Supportive Communication

Chapter 11: Motivation and Encouragement

Chapter 12: Handling Conflicts

CHAPTER 10

Supportive Communication

THE WAY WE TALK to our kids has a significant impact on their **learning** and ability to **listen** to us. We are constantly modeling behavior for our kids on how to act and behave. The way we talk to them also fits into this category. The way we speak to them and those around us is showing them how we want them to talk to us. I've found that there are three different ways that parents communicate with their kids:

The first one is **aggressive**. These parents yell a lot, put their kids down, and use attacking words. Their children respond in many ways including feeling fearful, yelling back and ignoring their parents' constant orders. This type of communication is associated with the **Authoritarian Parenting Style.**

The second form of communication seen is a **passive** form. These parents mutter, using soft, cautious words and tones when addressing their kids. In response, they often find that kids will ignore them or take advantage of them. Unfortunately, these parents are so passive that sometimes when they're pushed to their limits, they suddenly turn their communication into an aggressive tone. The passive form of communication is associated with the **Permissive Parenting Style**.

Finally, the third way that parents can communicate with their kids is by being **assertive**. This is what I've found to be by far the most effective way to interact with kids at all levels. An assertive way of communicating is firm, consistent, clear, positive, warm, and confident. Assertively communicating with kids is a real skill. It also demonstrates to your kids that mom and dad know what they're talking about and indicates to your child that they should listen and pay attention. This form of communication is associated with the **Authoritative Parenting Style**.

Here Are My Top Tips for Improving the WAY We Talk to Our Kids:

Use your child's name. Hearing your own name is music to your ears. Our kids are no different, plus it helps to get their attention before delivering your message, e.g., "George, please go and get…" Young children can often only concentrate on one thing at a time. Call your child's name and make sure you have their attention before you speak. For example, wait until he stops kicking the ball and looks at you. Then say, "George, lunch will be ready in ten minutes."

Use positive language. Try to avoid using words such as "no" or "don't" too often. When you say things like, "Don't drop that glass," "No running inside," or "Don't drag your coat in the dirt," you're doing two things: using negative language and putting the image of the action you don't want your child to take in their mind. This may cause them to accidentally do exactly what you told them not to, such as drop the glass.

Instead, try telling your kids what you want them to do, instead of what you don't want them to do. For example, try saying "Only walking inside please," or "Hold onto that glass, it's a special one," or "Hold the coat up, so it doesn't drag." This requires much thought and practice but is well worth the effort.

Try to eliminate words you use that may be ridiculing ("You're being a big baby."), name-calling ("You're a really bad boy.") and shaming ("You did a terrible thing."). This type of language achieves very little, other than leaving your child feeling worthless.

Kids will often cut off communication with those who use these words with them and begin to develop a poor self-image. Positive and kind words give your child more confidence, make them feel happier, help them behave better, and encourage them to try hard and achieve success. They learn to imitate you, and in turn, deliver the same respect and praise to others.

Examples of positive words are:

- "I like the way you remembered to pick up your toys."

- "Thank you for helping me clean up this mess."

- "You tried so hard to share your things with your sister; it made me feel really happy."

Connect with Your Child Using Eye Contact. You may need to get down at their level or sit at the table with them. When you're talking with your kids, this also shows them what they should do. Not only is it good manners, but it also helps you to listen to each other. Say your child's name until they make eye contact, especially before giving them a direction. It's important that they give you their attention, and you should model the same behavior for them.

Listen Reflectively to Your Child. This means not only listening to learn what they are thinking but also to listen for feelings. Pay full attention to your child while they're speaking. Stop what you are doing. For younger children, you may need to bend down toward them, sit next to them, or sit on a couch directly facing them. Then as you listen to your child's words, ask yourself, "How is my child feeling right now?" What are they trying to tell me? Finally, try to restate what you just heard conveying not only your understanding of their words but your impression of how they feel. You try to function as a mirror accurately reflecting their communication.

Here are some examples:

- "Sounds like you're feeling disappointed that Jane isn't coming to your birthday party."

- "Okay, I get it. You're angry because your little brother just broke your toy truck."

- "Seems like you're feeling lonesome since we moved, and wish your friends were closer."

Validate Your Child's Feelings. When children are unhappy, angry or frustrated, parents often attempt to minimize or redirect feelings.

Some examples include:

- "It's no big deal—you'll be fine."

- "These things just happen sometimes, you don't need to cry about it."

- "You shouldn't let things like that upset you so much. Sometimes we just need to let things go."

Instead, we should communicate that we understand how they feel and that it's understandable why they feel the way they do. You can combine the validation of feelings with reflective listening. Using the reflective listening examples above, here's how it might sound:

- "Sounds like you're feeling disappointed that Jane is not coming to your birthday party. I know she's your best friend and I understand why that might make you sad."

- "Okay, I get it. You're angry because your little brother just broke your toy truck. I understand why you're so upset. When you're feeling better, we can think of a way to solve the problem."

- "Seems like you're feeling lonesome since we moved, and wish your friends were closer. I know the move has been hard for you as you had many close friends there."

Sometimes we see how children are feeling by their facial gestures or their actions. This is very common with younger children in particular. A helpful approach is to associate their feelings with a word. You might say, "It looks to me like you're feeling (angry, bored, disappointed, frustrated, hurt). Would you like to talk about how you're feeling right now? I'd be happy to listen."

Be aware of how you're feeling as well. It may provide an opening for a problem-solving conversation, but if a child seems overly upset, it's best to have that talk at another time.

Sometimes, a look of concern and understanding, a hug or just sitting quietly and listening is the most helpful thing you can do for the moment.

Use I-Messages Instead of You-Messages

You-messages often come across as nagging, blaming, or as a put down.

- "You know better than that."
- "When are you going to get around to cleaning your room?"
- "You never listen to me."

I-messages allow you to convey how you feel but in a more positive way. They also show respect. Parents are less likely to be tuned out by their kids when they use I-messages. I-messages can be a simple request or praise, but they also can express how you're feeling about a particular issue. When they're used for the latter, they often have three components:

When they are used for the latter, they often have three components:

1. When
2. I feel
3. Because

    - "When you leave your toys all over the floor, I worry because someone might trip and get hurt or step on a toy and break it."
    - "When you come home late and don't call me, I feel scared because I think you might have been in an accident."

They can be used to give praise and support.

    - "I really feel good when I come home to a neat house."

- Even better is the use of descriptive praise. "I really feel good when I come home and see that clothes are hung up and there are no snack wrappers on the floor."

- You can simply say, "I love you so much," or "I am so proud of how well you are doing in school."

Open communication is so important. My favorite books on communicating with kids are the following:

- How to Talk so Kids Will Listen & Listen so Kids Will Talk by Adele Faber and Elaine Mazlish

- How to Talk so Little Kids Will Listen: A Survival Guide to Life with Children Ages 2-7 by Joanna Faber and Julie King

- How to Talk So Teens Will Listen and Listen So Teens Will Talk by Adele Faber and Elaine Mazlish

CHAPTER 11

Motivation and Encouragement

How to Encourage Your Child to Feel Important

IT'S IMPERATIVE FOR A child's healthy development that they feel important and worthy. Healthy self-esteem is a child's armor against the challenges of the world. Kids who feel good about themselves seem to have an easier time handling conflicts and resisting negative pressures.

They tend to smile more readily and enjoy life. These kids are realistic and are more likely to be optimistic. Research shows that children who feel important are well-rounded, respectful, and excel in academics, extracurricular activities, and hobbies. They are also more likely to develop healthy relationships with their peers.

In contrast, challenges can become sources of major anxiety and frustration for children who don't feel important or cherished. Children who think poorly of themselves have a hard time solving problems and may become passive, withdrawn and depressed.

You are the biggest influence in terms of your child feeling important, valued and worthy. Remember to praise your child for a job well done, as well as for putting forth a valiant effort. Praise the good traits they naturally possess and help them find ways to learn from their mistakes and failures. Be honest and sincere in your praise. Help your kids realize that you also suffer from self-doubt and can make mistakes from time to time, but that you know that you're important, valued and loved.

Three factors affect an individual's level of motivation: competence, autonomy, and relatedness. Each of these is a basic need for human beings, and whether they are met or frustrated will affect that person's motivation. Competence is the drive to feel able and successful. Autonomy means having control of your own life–being able to "be yourself." Relatedness is the human need to interact with others and form relationships. Parents build up their children's self-esteem and self-worth by providing appropriate praise, giving proper levels of responsibility for the child's age and developmental stage, and by showing unconditional love and positive regard. Each of these is closely related to the needs for competence, autonomy, and relatedness.

When a child receives praise for doing well, this meets their need for competence. That's why it's vital not to over-praise, or to say a child has done well when it's clear they haven't. A child who is unsure whether or not praise is genuine will find it more difficult to satisfy the need for competence in later life. You need to be clear that you're praising the child, not the action. If a child brings you a drawing, telling them, "You're very good at drawing," builds esteem and meets the need for competence in a way that, "It's a very good drawing," does not.

Children need appropriate levels of responsibility. This can vary from asking a toddler to "help" with putting away the groceries, to allowing an older child to walk home with friends, to permitting your teenage son to choose a color scheme for his bedroom. Giving children a chance to feel in control will build self-esteem and meet their need for autonomy.

Motivation to achieve seems to come from self-esteem, rather than self-esteem coming from achievement. Edward Deci and Richard Ryan, two of the leading figures in self-determination theory, looked at whether reaching goals builds up a sense of self-worth. If this were the case, then the most successful individuals should also be the happiest. In fact, Deci and Ryan found that self-esteem based on achievements tends to be more fragile. People who base their sense of self-worth on what they have achieved need more reassurance and compare themselves more with others. Children who learn that their worth comes from what they have done, rather than who they are, will be more likely to develop into insecure adults.

Sometimes children need to be told what to do. This is extrinsic motivation, but it can become internalized. At some point, every parent has responded to a child's question, "Why do I have to do this?" with "Because I said so!" But a child who cleans his room because he is told to do so may find that he enjoys having a neat and organized space and can feel a sense of accomplishment for finishing the task. Parents might state the benefits of a specific task or accomplishment to help a child recognize and appreciate the benefits of his actions. Over time, he may see himself as a well-organized person, meeting his need for autonomy (being himself) by cleaning up after himself. This is still an extrinsic motivation. Few children will clean their room for the love of the activity, but the more it is internalized, the more the child can meet those basic needs and develop genuine self-worth.

Every parent wants their child to be happy and to try their best. Again, self-determination theory shows that children who meet their needs for competence, autonomy, and relatedness will feel good about themselves, and will thus gain motivation to develop, grow and succeed.

Here are some steps you can take to help your child develop confidence and competence:

Set Goals. Help them to make a list of goals. From the list discuss together the desirability and feasibility of each. Start with one long-term goal and then add a few short-term goals that will help your child achieve the long-term goal. Help your child develop a timeline and decide who and/or what might help them reach the goal.

Celebrate Accomplishments. When your child accomplishes goals, let them know how proud you are of them. Cheer them on as they move toward a goal. For the achievement of a long-term goal, hold a celebration event of some kind. Maybe you go out for a meal or go to a local amusement spot such as riding go-carts or playing miniature golf.

Play the Role of a Coach. Let them know you are there to help them. Discuss their progress. If they run into an obstacle, problem solve together. It's important to teach your child how to do a root cause analysis of a problem. Help them brainstorm possible solutions. Teach your child how to go on the Internet to look for answers to their problem. Help them look at the pros and cons for each and select one to try out.

Provide Encouragement. If your child becomes discouraged, help them learn how to shift from negative thoughts to positive thoughts. Let them know that most people feel discouraged from time to time—even star athletes and entertainers. Help your child to come up with a positive affirmation statement they can use to keep them going.

Teach Your Child Resiliency with These Tips

Every parent wants their child to be resilient. Ask any child psychology or child development expert how valuable resiliency is, and he or she will confirm that it's significant.

First, let's look at what being resilient means. In basic terms, being resilient means the ability to rebound or spring back to original form. Of course, we as parents want to shield and protect our children from every mishap and hurt, but this isn't realistic. As children mature, especially during pubescent and adolescent years, we should take a step back and bite our tongue as we painfully watch our children maneuver their way through this tough time. However, if we step in and act for them, take on their battles, and defend them, we do not allow them the freedom and the space to grow.

In *Building Resilience in Children and Teens: Giving Kids Roots and Wings*, published in 2011 by the American Academy of Pediatrics, the author, Kenneth Ginsburg, M.D. lists the seven "Cs" of resilience: Competence, Confidence, Connection, Character, Contribution, Coping, and Control.

Competence is a feeling that you know how to handle situations when they occur. You can help children to feel competent by focusing on their unique strengths. If they made a mistake in handling a problem, relate it to that specific situation. "You made a bad decision that time, but you're not a bad person. We all make mistakes, and we need to see them as learning opportunities". Look for opportunities to let your child make decisions.

Children develop **confidence** by accepting and owning their actions that reflect competence. Point out and describe specific incidents in which your child demonstrated competence in handling a particular situation. Help them to learn to recognize when they have done well. Encourage your child to tap into the good feelings that come from accomplishing a goal or a task. While being encouraging, monitor your input to be sure you're not pushing them beyond their capabilities or resources.

Connection through a supportive family provides a sense of security and acceptance. Open communication within the family also gives a child or teen a place where they can share their thoughts and feelings, seek guidance, and ask for help if needed. This also serves as a safe place for a child facing a tense or hostile situation at school or in the neighborhood.

Family meetings and open communication, during which parents impart values and morals, helps build strong **character** in children and teens. This also helps them to become caring individuals in their community and makes it easier for them to make difficult choices and feel confident they did the right thing.

Discussing the value of and need for generosity, as well as demonstrating generosity yourself, will help your child to look for opportunities to **contribute** in some way. Donating time to a community project or participating in a fundraising event as a family is a great way to model and teach the importance of contributing to the community and enables them to experience the positive feelings that accompany the act of contribution. Your family could join an organized activity such as a walk to raise funds or a beach or park clean-up event.

Look for opportunities to help your child develop **coping** skills. When they're stressed, show them how using mindfulness can help them cope. Demonstrate positive coping skills when you're dealing with a stressful situation or share past experiences about how you managed to cope and how good it felt when you were able to handle it appropriately.

I highly recommend Dr. Ginzburg's book as a valuable addition to your parenting resource library.

Look for "teachable moments" when your child has made a mistake or poor choice, to help them realize how they can learn to stop and think before reacting to a situation or engaging in inappropriate behavior. This puts them in **control** of their actions by using their capacity to think, and problem solve rather than yielding to their emotions. Help your child understand that emotions are a state of being, not a personal trait. They can learn how to tame their emotions and unleash their problem-solving skills.

Here are several ways to teach your child how to be resilient during tough times:

Talk It Out. Show your child that you know how bad they feel by being empathetic. Let them know that you're there to talk it out, and also to listen. Make sure your child knows that no one gets through any stage of life unscathed–it's a rite of passage on the way to becoming a mature adult. If your child knows that you care and are always willing to listen to them talk about their struggles, he or she will bounce back a lot quicker than going it alone.

Give Them Some Space. Make sure to give your child the space he needs to figure things out on his own. Sometimes, as parents, we want to fix our child's problems, make it all better, or just make it go away. However, when we do this, we don't offer our child the opportunity to become resilient.

Learning that falls, trip-ups, setbacks, and mistakes are all a part of life doesn't mean that it has to be the whole of life. Learning that you survive, people forget, and that you can laugh at yourself later on in life are all tools to help your child move on. Give them space to figure it out on their own. Let them know that you're there for them while giving them some elbow room.

Teach Them How to Laugh. One of the best ways to gain resiliency is to point out that one day they will look back and have the ability to put things in perspective. Teach them that sometimes they may need to chalk it up to being human and, as a human, it's about making and learning from mistakes. Let them know that it's okay to laugh at yourself later down the road. Teach them that it will get better.

One of the best ways to get them to laugh is to relate a story of yours when you were younger, and things did not go as planned. Show your child that not only did you survive, but you thrived instead. Point out situations where famous athletes and musicians were laughed at or made fun of, told they would never make it, and then went on to succeed above and beyond their wildest dreams.

Teach Mindfulness Meditation to Children

Mindfulness meditation is practiced sitting while cross-legged on a cushion with your back straight and eyes closed. Attention is put on the movement of the abdomen when breathing in and out, or on the awareness of the breath as it goes in and out the nostrils. As thoughts come up, return to focusing on breathing. Meditators start with short periods of 10 minutes or so a day. As you practice regularly, it becomes easier to keep attention focused on breathing. Eventually, awareness of breath will extend into awareness of thoughts, feelings, and actions.

If you're already into practicing mindfulness, you know the emotional and spiritual benefits of living in the moment, and now you want to teach mindfulness meditation to your kids as well. Here's how. The way you learned mindfulness meditation would probably not work for your child. You can't expect her to sit cross-legged, close her eyes and watch her thoughts flow by without being judgmental. If you ask her to do all these, you might only succeed in putting her off mindfulness meditation for the rest of her life. You'll need to teach mindfulness meditation to your kid in a way that she finds enjoyable enough to tear herself away from the computer.

Most children find it difficult to understand abstract concepts. Ensure that you give clear, concise, and detailed instructions when you guide them through mindfulness exercises. Children enjoy participating in activities that allow them to be imaginative and creative. Keep this in mind when creating the activities.

The easiest way to initiate a child into the practice of mindfulness is to make him more aware of his immediate environment and the objects in it. Ask your kid to draw a common household object from memory. Once the picture is complete, ask him to observe the object minutely for a period of time. You may want to guide him by pointing out the little details on the object, such as its texture or markings. Ask him to draw the object again and compare the two drawings.

You can carry out similar exercises with an animated movie or a book with older kids. You can ask them to describe the attire of a particular character or list the characters present in a scene after they have watched the film or read the book for the first time. You can add novelty to the mindfulness practice routine by asking them to write down the objects they see and the people they meet on their way to and from school.

Kids are often more mindful than most adults. Your child doesn't have much of a past to ruminate upon, and she'll undoubtedly be the last person to worry about an uncertain future. Teaching her to become aware of her immediate environment with fun exercises will teach her to live in the present moment. Eventually, this habit will help her graduate with ease to advanced mindfulness meditation practices, such as becoming aware of her body and emotions.

Here are a few simple stress reduction techniques that are easy and effective for children, teens, and adults:

My favorite is the **5-Minute-Vacation.** Close your eyes and take a few deep breaths. Then visualize a favorite place or activity. Let your imagination carry you away to a special spot that is relaxing and refreshing. See everything there is to see. Hear everything there is to hear. Feel everything there is to feel.

Help your child learn to view mental pictures in their head, such as:

Multiple Animals. If your child likes animals, ask her to tell which ones she likes best. Ask her to picture herself sitting with a puppy (or whatever animal she enjoys). Ask her to close her eyes and to feel the puppy's soft fur and see its color. She can have the puppy be any color and type she wants. She can also have more than one puppy. She can sit and pet or play with the puppy.

Favorite Activity. Ask your child what he likes to do. Then say, "Imagine that you can see yourself doing that. Let yourself really enjoy it". Some possibilities could be playing a musical instrument, riding a bike, riding a horse, playing on the slide at the playground or playing a video game.

Cloud Gazing. "What are some colors you like? Good. Let yourself imagine some beautiful clouds in the sky and see them change into one of your favorite colors. Good. Now let them change into another color or perhaps several nice colors. The clouds may change shape, too, as you continue to watch them. It will be interesting to see what they become. You can be part of those clouds, if you like, feeling very comfortable, very good."

Favorite Song. "I know you like to sing. Where do you like to do that best? Good. Imagine that you are there now, singing your favorite song. Sing the song through in your mind. Enjoy doing it very well, making just the sounds you like."

Listen to Music. "I know you like listening to music. What is your favorite song? Just imagine yourself hearing that very clearly now, as loud or soft as you like. You may imagine watching the musicians too, including your favorite singers." You may even let your child listen to a recording at first and then later hear it in her mind.

Sports Activity. "I know you like to play football. Imagine yourself at the age you are now or older playing on your favorite football team, wearing its uniform, playing the position you like. Let yourself get very comfortable as you imagine a game with your team winning. You're helping your team win. Feel your control as your muscles move the way you tell them, running or throwing or kicking. Enjoy being with the winning team and continue until you win the game."

Teaching kids and teens to become self-motivated and develop resiliency is a process. Look for "teachable moments." Coaching these skills will improve the likelihood that they will retain the "lesson. Having them practice during "in the moment" will facilitate brain development through adding or strengthening circuits. Also, practicing these skills during family meeting periodically helps to reinforce the learning.

American Psychological Association, *Resilience Guide for Parents and Teachers*, is a great online resource. [www.apa.org/helpcenter/resilience.aspx] as well as the book *Building Resilience in Children and Teens: Giving Kids Roots and Wings*, by Dr. Kenneth Ginsburg.

CHAPTER 12

Handling Conflicts

RELATIONSHIPS ARE MADE UP of two or more individuals with different temperaments and personalities. As a result, disagreements are going to occur. It's not a matter of if a problem will arise, but how to solve it together when it does. In this section, we will examine how to resolve conflicts with other family members, including you and your partner, inter-sibling conflict, and disagreements between you and your children.

How to Cope with a Disagreement with Your Partner

Take a Break. There is great wisdom in the advice of stopping and counting to 10 when you're angry. This buys you time to avoid a quick reaction that can inflame the situation. Taking a break can be, "I think I need to take a walk to settle down," or "Let me just have some time to myself and let's come back and work on this." This does NOT mean storming out or avoiding the problem altogether. It's a cooling-down period to hopefully usher in reason and logic as opposed to reaction and anger.

See the Other Side. Once the strong feelings have settled, take a moment to try and view the situation through the eyes and heart of the person with whom you're arguing. If you do this consistently, in time, you will grow to understand the person instead of being inclined to attack them. This takes practice, which requires a decision and a choice. If you keep at it, eventually it will become a positive habit.

Find Common Ground. Think about the things you agree on and in which you can find commonality. If you can outweigh the negative thoughts with positive ones, you will find it much easier to resolve your conflict. You can start to remind each other that you're partners rather than enemies.

Really Listen. It's natural to want to explain your side, be defensive and shut off listening to your partner. However, this only alienates and causes hard feelings. Both of you need to sit back and absorb what the other person is saying. Ask questions about their point of view. Repeat to them what they're saying to clarify if you understand correctly. This will take the conflict from hostile back to a place where you care what the other person is thinking and feeling.

Compromise When Possible. If possible, compromise and negotiate. There are times when too much is at stake to give up your position and find a middle ground, but most of the time, it's quite manageable to find a solution that can eventually work for everyone. Work together to find a way for everyone to feel that the outcome is reasonable.

Let It Go. If you have gotten caught up in a mess that seems impossible to resolve, decide to end it immediately. If you conflict with someone who is important to you, remind yourself that the relationship is worth more than being right. Forgive each other and move on. It's rarely worth winning an argument if you damage a significant relationship in the process.

It's essential to understand that not all couple issues can quickly resolve. A qualified counselor can help to provide tools and strategies that bring you both back onto safe and common ground. You're a work in progress and the time spent on nurturing your healthy relationships will be worth it in the end.

Tips for Becoming a Peaceful and Calm Parent

Anger and frustration are universal human emotions, but that doesn't mean you have to be a victim of negative feelings. As adults, we have an obligation to our family and ourselves to avoid allowing our emotions from getting the best of us.

Let's face it. Parenting is tough! When you simply want to pee alone or take a shower for more than two minutes without hearing little footsteps outside the curtain, it can be incredibly frustrating. Or, when you've told your child for the gazillionth time to turn off the light when they leave a room, it can make you want to pull your hair out.

One way that many parents express their anger and frustration is by yelling at their kids. It's not because they want to necessarily, but because sometimes they get so overwhelmed, they lose control. Other times it may just be easier to holler than to learn strategies to become a calmer parent.

Studies show that yelling makes children more aggressive, physically and verbally. As a parent, raising your voice to the point of screaming scares children and makes them feel insecure. It has been shown to cause long-term effects, such as anxiety, low self-esteem, and increased aggression. A parent who is calm is reassuring, which makes children feel loved and accepted in spite of bad behavior.

There are many responses you can choose when faced with a situation that makes your blood boil. Finding peace is possible! Learn to manage your anger and arrive at a peaceful solution using these strategies:

Consider the Negative Consequences of Expressing Anger. It's tempting to run with your exasperation in the short-term but giving in to rage can cause even more challenges. Before lashing out at your kids or taking what you believe to be appropriate actions, consider how things will be when the smoke clears.

Give Yourself a Timeout. Timeouts aren't just for young kids. Adults also need timeouts or short breaks to calm down. Taking deep breaths, give yourself a few minutes to allow a level of reason to return to your mind. You'll be in a better place to make appropriate parenting decisions.

When Appropriate, Let Your Family Members Be Wrong. Even though you might have a strong opinion on a particular topic, it's okay to listen and ask questions to understand better where they are coming from. You might even be surprised that through that approach they might ask for your thoughts. You could then let them know that you understand their point of view and that it's normal for people to have opposing points of view and accept and respect them. You could then share your thoughts as just one way to look at a particular issue.

Take a Minute to Notice Your Anger. Instead of mindlessly reacting to your frustration, take a moment to examine it. Pretend you're a third-party witnessing your irritation and annoyance. What does it feel like to you? Where is the emotion coming from in your body? Is the feeling in your head, chest, or stomach? Has your breathing changed? Are your hands shaking or clenching? By disengaging from your anger, you can gain a different perspective and weaken your negative emotions.

Ask Yourself Why You're Upset. Did someone physically harm you? Did they let you down? Violate one of your values? Figure out why you're frustrated, and you'll be able to take the necessary steps to discover a solution.

Focus on the Big Picture. Imagine that you knew the world would come to an end next Friday. Would you be upset if your child didn't hang his backpack? Of course not.

Look for Solutions, rather than trying to make yourself feel better. Acting in anger is about making yourself feel better. Rather than yelling at your kids, for instance, work on finding a peaceful solution. The outcome will be much better and well worth your time.

Be Sure You Understand the Situation. Why get angry with your kids before you know the facts? Ensure the issue isn't a possible miscommunication.

Learn and Practice Relaxation Techniques. The more relaxed you are on a regular basis as a parent, the less likely you are to become angry. Relaxation techniques can also be helpful after the fact. Learn how to self-soothe. It's a skill that can be learned.

See Your Annoyance as a Practice Opportunity to Find Peace. Each time you feel upset, view the situation as a chance to practice your anger-management skills. It's a blessing in disguise. Commit yourself to manage this bout of frustration better than you did the last time.

Avoid letting anger, frustration, and annoyance get the best of you. As a thoughtful, loving human being and parent, you have options available to you. Pause and take a few deep breaths and let it go. Ask questions, so you're better able to understand your child's point of view. Do some problem-solving. Seek to find solutions and peace rather than giving in to your immediate impulses.

Empathy: Teaching Kids to Value Others. Empathy is one of those strange qualities– something almost everyone wants, but few know how to truly give or receive. In a world where a huge emphasis is on self-gratification, it's in short supply but high demand. This is all the more reason to teach the next generation what it means to have empathy for those around them.

What Is Empathy? Many people confuse sympathy and empathy, but they're two distinct values. Empathy isn't just the ability to understand someone's feelings–criminals often take advantage of people by appearing to understand their feelings and subsequently gaining their trust. Empathy is more than that. Not only is it the ability to recognize how someone feels, but it also values and respects the feelings of another person. It means treating others with kindness, dignity, and understanding.

Kids Need to See Adults Show Empathy. While some children are gifted with naturally kind hearts, in most cases, kids need to see empathy modeled by the adults around them. It begins with the way parents relate to their children. Parents who show an interest in the things that matter to their kids and respond to emotions in a positive and caring way are teaching the skill of empathy.

Meet Emotional Needs. When children have their emotional needs met, two things happen. They learn how to meet the emotional needs of others and they are anchored in what they are receiving, meaning they are secure enough to give to others when the need arises. But first they need to receive—an empty jug cannot fill a cup.

Talk to Kids about Emotional Needs. Many adults find it difficult to talk about emotional needs or anything related to feelings. Consequently, they spend their lives tiptoeing around the subject. These are people who don't know how to handle the emotions of others and are uncomfortable with any situation that calls for an emotional response. Sometimes they're afraid of their feelings because they've never learned how to deal with emotional needs.

It's a good idea to talk to kids about emotions and how other people experience them. Give their feelings names (for example, jealousy, anger, and love) and teach them that these are normal. Talk to your children about how to handle emotions positively and point out situations where other people are experiencing feelings. Teach them about respecting the feelings of others and show them how to act in a situation where a response is required.

Look for Real Life Situations to Practice Empathy. There's nothing like a real-life example to model what you're teaching. Look for situations that affect another person and talk to your kids about what it means to the people involved and how they might feel. For example, if you see an ambulance speed past, talk about how the family members of the sick person might be feeling.

Play Games. Younger kids in particular love to pretend that they're someone or something else. You can use these fun times for teaching empathy. Get your kids playing the role of another person. This might be a character in a book or on TV, or even someone you know who has been through a significant experience lately. You can act out the story together and ask your kids to stop and imagine how their character might have been feeling at any given moment. This will focus their attention on the emotions that another person might experience when in that situation. You can ask them to make faces that reflect the feelings of their character.

Develop Their Inner Moral Compass. Teaching your kids the difference between right and wrong from a young age gives them a strong internal moral compass that will direct them to make good choices. In situations that require a decision, help them to see how our choices and behavior affect others. Talk to them about how wrongdoings harms people and help them to understand the hurt and damage it causes. It's a good idea to talk to them about the little things, such as calling a sibling an unkind name that hurts her feelings or refusing to play with their brother when friends visit. When building a strong moral foundation, start small and begin with the basics.

Empathetic Kids: Givers Not Takers. By raising your kids to understand and practice empathy, you're giving them the gift of giving. In a world where great emphasis is on looking out for one's own interests, people who are givers are all too rare. But they are the ones who enjoy the greatest satisfaction from life, have the most meaningful experiences, and are involved in more rewarding relationships. Teaching your kids empathy is a worthwhile investment for their futures and the world they will inhabit.

Teaching Conflict Resolution to Your Children. Children will be children. And if you have more than one in a room, there's a good bet there will be an argument or conflict at some point. Teaching conflict resolution to your children will reduce your frustrations and help bring peace to your home. One way to address conflict resolution is by using books. Authors of children's books can write to a child's level of understanding. They create characters that children can identify with. The story can be used to describe a conflict between characters as well as demonstrate to children the best way to resolve that conflict. Once they see a different approach to solve problems, they'll be more likely to use those skills the next time they have an issue. While you're reading the story to your children, occasionally stop to discuss what's going on.

Ask them questions such as:

- Have you ever felt that way?

- What have you done in a similar situation in the past?

- How do you think _____ feels about what happened to them?

- What do you think _____ is going to do?

- What would you do?

Continue reading the story and talking about what's going on in it. Help your kids understand there are two sides to every argument or conflict. Ask them about their feelings and how these feelings might affect what they say or do. You could also ask them how they might resolve what's going on in the story before you read that part. Finally, ask them what the character learned from the situation in the book and how that knowledge could help them to solve their own conflicts.

Talk about appropriate ways to handle conflicts. Remind them never to use violence because violence never solves a problem–it only creates other problems. Help them see that talking about an issue and working toward a resolution together is the best way to resolve a conflict.

With younger children, try using puppets for stuffed animals to act out the situation or incident under discussion. Take turns playing the different roles. With my own children, and during play therapy sessions with patients, it was always amazing to see how this increases empathy as well as how others see them. This usually leads to a problem-solving discussion and the opportunity to teach valuable interpersonal relationship skills.

Do your best to be a good role model for your children. If you live with other people, you're going to have a conflict sooner or later. Remember that your children are watching you. They want to see how you handle disputes, even with them—especially once you start teaching them about it. If you get angry, yell and shout, they're less likely to believe that's not the right way to solve a problem. Try to remain calm and talk about things rather than letting your emotions get the best of you.

Here are some steps you may want to model for your kids:

- When you begin feeling angry or frustrated, stop before you say something you'll regret.

- Take a deep breath and count to ten.

- Calmly explain how you feel about what happened or was said.

- Listen to what the other person has to say about the subject.

- Think about different solutions to the problem.

- If you can't reach an agreement which both of you can accept, ask someone who isn't involved to help you resolve the conflict. Agree to abide by what is suggested.

Once you begin teaching conflict resolution to your children, you may notice less stress and fussing in your home. Continue to work with them when they have disagreements, model conflict resolution before them, and your children will be better equipped to handle any conflicts they have in the future. And isn't that what parenting is all about—equipping our children for life outside of the home?

Handling Sibling Rivalry. It seems strange that whenever the word "sibling" comes up, "rivalry" seems sure to follow, even though there are many stable sibling relationships in families (brothers and sisters who genuinely like and enjoy one another). However, it's typically rivalry that gets the most attention.

What causes sibling rivalry? Think about it. Siblings don't choose the family they're born into, nor do they pick each other. They may be of different genders, probably of different ages and temperaments, and worst of all, they have to share the one or two people they want most for themselves: their parents. Other factors which may cause sibling rivalry include:

- **Position in the Family.** For example, the oldest child may have the burden of responsibilities for the younger children, or the younger child spends his life trying to catch up with an older sibling.

- **Gender.** For instance, a son may resent his sister because his father seems gentler with her. On the other hand, a daughter may wish she could go on the fishing trip with her father and brother.

- **Age.** A five and an eight-year-old can play some games together, but when they become ten and thirteen, they will likely have very different interests.

The most important factor, however, is a parent's attitude. Parents have been taught that they must be impartial with their kids, but this can be extremely difficult. It's inevitable that parents will feel differently about children who have their own personalities with varying needs, dispositions, and places in the family. Picture the age-old conflict of the young child whining: "It's not fair. Why can't I stay up until nine-thirty like Johnny?" Fairness has nothing to do with it. Susie is younger and needs more sleep. It's as simple as that, and parents are advised never to give in to the old "it's not fair" strategy. Besides, when Susie is finally allowed to stay up until nine-thirty, it will feel like a privilege to her.

Many parents feel that to be fair, they must treat their children equally. It's not possible and can be dehumanizing if a mother feels that when she hugs one child, she must stop and hug all of her children. Over time, hugs will eventually become somewhat meaningless in that family. When Susie has a birthday or is ill, she is the one who merits the special attention and presents. You can be sure that no matter what they may say, the other children in the family recognize the inherent "fairness" of the situation.

Ever since we decided that sibling rivalry is a typical occurrence in a family system, we've had a terrible time figuring out what to do about it. Here are some "do's and don'ts" that may be helpful in reducing conflicts as well as the negative effects of sibling rivalry:

- **Don't Make Comparisons** (e.g., "I don't understand it. When Johnny was his age, he could already tie his shoes."). Each child feels he is unique and rightly so; he is his own person and resents being evaluated only in relation to someone else. Instead of comparison, each child in the family should have his own goals and levels of expectation that relate only to him.

- **Don't Dismiss or Suppress Your Children's Resentment or Angry Feelings.** Contrary to what many people think, anger is not something we should try to avoid at all costs. It's an entirely normal part of being human, and it's certainly normal for siblings to get angry with each other and have the impulse to fight physically. They need the adults in their lives to assure them that mothers and fathers get mad too but have learned self-control, and that angry feelings do not give license to behave in cruel and dangerous ways. This is the time to sit down, acknowledge the anger (e.g., "I know you hate David right now, but you cannot hit him with a stick."), and talk it through. You can use opportunities like this to review the "Stop, Breathe, Problem Solve" method of conflict resolution. Help them to evaluate possible solutions assessing the pros and cons of each.

- **Try to Avoid Situations That Promote Guilt in Siblings.** First, we must teach children that feelings and actions are not synonymous. It may be normal to want to hit the baby on the head, but parents must stop a child from doing it. The guilt that follows doing something mean is a lot worse than the guilt of merely feeling mean. In situations like this, parental intervention must be quick and decisive.

Some Useful Sibling Conflict Resolution Strategies

Common Mistakes Parents Make in Managing Sibling Rivalry:

Taking Sides, such as attempting to punish the child who is at fault, (usually the one seen pounding on the other child). How long has this child put up with the taunting of the other child before taking drastic measures? If you attempt to assign blame in a situation like this, 50% of the time you will be wrong.

Ignoring Appropriate Behavior. Parents often ignore their children when they're playing nicely. They only pay attention when a problem arises. Behavior Mod 101 teaches that behaviors that are unnoticed (go unrewarded) decrease while behaviors that receive attention (are rewarded) increase. Look for opportunities to "catch them being good."

Simple Parenting Techniques That Work

When the sibling rivalry progresses to excessive physical or verbal violence OR when the number of incidents of rivalry becomes excessive, take action. (Action does speak louder than words). Talk with your children about what is going on. Provide suggestions on how they can handle the situation when it occurs, such as:

- Ignoring the teasing.

- Simply agreeing (in a kidding way) that whatever the teaser is saying is true.

- Telling the teaser that "enough is enough."

- When these measures aren't working, ask the person in charge (parent, babysitter) for help.

When the above does not work, introduce a family plan to help with the situation that provides negative and positive consequences for all concerned, such as:

- When there is any fighting or shouting, all involved will have a timeout or the temporary removal of screen time.

- However, when we can go the whole day or afternoon or evening (whatever makes sense for your situation) without fighting, everyone will earn a privilege such as

  - You can have a snack.

  - I will read you a story.

  - We will all play a game together.

  - I will play outside with you (catch, etc.)

  - You can stay up later.

  - (Note that several of these provide parental attention for appropriate behavior).

Develop a system for evenly distributing coveted privileges. In other words, a method for taking turns for such things as:

- Who gets to ride "shotgun" in the car? (It's amazing how many teenagers and young adult siblings still make this an important issue).

- Who gets to push the button in the elevator?

- Who gets to choose where to go to eat lunch or dinner?

- Who gets to choose the television show?

- Who does the dishes or takes out the trash? (Rotate on a weekly or monthly basis).

Yes, siblings can create certain stresses, but if they're overcome, they'll give your children resources that will serve them well later in life. Siblings learn how to share, how to come face to face with jealousy, and how to accept their individual strengths and weaknesses.

Best of all, as they watch you handle sibling rivalry with patience and fairness, they'll be gaining knowledge that will be valuable when they, too, become parents.

Section 2 – Open Communication - Summary

Ideas & Recommendations for Increasing Open Communication in Your Family

Suggested First Steps to Improving Communication in Your Family:

1. Make sure you're taking time to take care of yourself and work on your relationship with your partner.

2. Periodically review the guidelines for supportive communication in Chapter 10 on your own and with your partner. Reflect on your progress.

    a. What techniques have you been using?

    b. Are they working?

    c. What techniques might you add to your skill set?

    d. Consider checking out the recommendations for Chapters 10–12 in the Resource Section for more suggestions.

3. When conflicts arise, consider using problem-solving either as a family or just with the individual directly involved. Here are the basic steps:

    a. Define the problem. What happens? Why is it a problem? When does it happen? How often does it happen?

    b. Get "buy-in" from all concerned that the problem needs a resolution.

    c. Brainstorm possible solutions. Don't judge–just make a list.

    d. Go over the solutions generated during the brainstorming session and look at the pros and cons of each.

    e. Select a solution you think will work. Develop a plan and give it a try.

    f. Keep track of success. Change your approach if necessary.

g. You can use the Family Problem Solving Contract as a tool to implement the solution.

h. For more help, check out the information on Collaborative Problem Solving found at *ThinkKids.org*

4. Motivation can be facilitated by praise and in some cases reward. See the Words of Encouragement & Praise and the Reward Suggestions charts for some guidance.

5. If your child is having trouble responding appropriately to reasonable requests for action, consider using the One-Time Club chart.

   a. Explain the importance of following directions and explain that the chart will help them learn how to become an expert at this skill.

   b. Place a star or happy face in a square each time your child follows a direction on the first request and give them praise.

   c. When all the squares have been filled, hold a graduation session and provide a previously agreed upon reward.

   d. Continue to give praise occasionally when they comply with a request the first time.

6. Take a look at the I Can Pledge and HOME chart. Consider reviewing these at each family meeting. Discuss how well EVERYONE is doing. Review each element of HOME and provide examples of success and room for improvement.

Tools for Success: Open Communication

Family Problem Solving Contract. This is a tool to help resolve problems between family members. It will usually apply for parent/child issues, but it could be used for parent/parent issues as well.

- When you become aware of a repeated issue (such as not putting things away, sibling rivalry, not coming home on time, not sharing, etc.), you should wait for a time when everyone involved is calm and free to talk.

- Open the session using "I messages" and stating your concerns (describing the behavior and why it is a problem for you).

- Ask the person to share their point of view and invite them to share in a brainstorming session to find a solution that would be okay with all.

- Brainstorm by writing down all ideas shared (do not judge them).

- Look at the pros and cons for each suggested solution.

- Decide to try one and write out the contract.

- Agree on a time to review progress and revise the plan if necessary or celebrate a solved problem.

Things I Can Do When I Am Bored. Some children have a more difficult time finding things to do than others. If you discover this is an issue, find a good time to discuss it with your child. Help them generate the list of activities. For younger children, you might want to find images on the Internet, print them and attach to a poster board. Remind your child when they feel bored to go and look at the list and select an activity to do.

HOME. This is a suggestion for coming up with a family pact on how you want to support and enjoy each other. It could be discussed and reviewed at your regular family meetings. You can certainly use this as a model and come up with your own. The affirmations might be written on a card for review by family members when they want to improve the way they relate to others or how they want to develop their own success in life.

First Time Club. This is a very useful tool to employ when a younger child either argues when given a reasonable request or they agree but do not follow through.

- Find a good time to discuss your concern.

- Obtain buy-in from your child.

- Set up the chart and agree on the reward for filling all the squares with a "happy face" or another symbol you and your child select.

- When your child follows directions after one request, praise and thank them and fill in one of the squares. If they require a reminder say, "Remember you're working to be a member of the 'First Time Club,' and you still need to do what I asked but remember next time to do what I asked right away. I know you can do that."

- Once the squares are filled, hold a celebration and provide the reward. From time to time provide praise and always provide a thank you.

Reward Ideas for Kids & Teens. From time to time, you may find that providing a reward for complying with a contract may be useful in giving the motivation to help your child learn a new behavior. Remember, the best way to eliminate an undesirable behavior is to replace it with new behavior.

Words of Encouragement and Praise. Encouragement and praise are essential in human relationships. For many, it seems more natural to complain about bothering behaviors rather than to praise, provide thanks, and encouragement for desirable behaviors. Try not commenting on minor annoyances and instead look for opportunities to praise positive behaviors. You'll be amazed with the results.

Please be sure to visit parentingtoday.com/tools for PDF versions of the charts provided at the end of each section as well as additional resources, including updates, classes, and forums for parents.

Things I Can Do When I Am Bored

Things I can do outside:
Toys I can play with:
Books I would like to read:
Art and other creative projects:
My favorite videos or music:
Other ideas:

First Time Club

_____ is working to become a member of the First Time Club. To become a member, you must be able to what you are asked right away the first time you are asked. Every time you do something the first time asked, a square on the chart will be filled with a _____. When ALL of the squares on the chart are filled, you will become a member of the club and receive _____

<table>
<tr><td></td><td></td><td></td><td></td><td></td></tr>
<tr><td></td><td></td><td></td><td></td><td></td></tr>
<tr><td></td><td></td><td></td><td></td><td></td></tr>
<tr><td></td><td></td><td></td><td></td><td></td></tr>
<tr><td></td><td></td><td></td><td></td><td></td></tr>
<tr><td></td><td></td><td></td><td></td><td></td></tr>
</table>

Reward Ideas for Kids and Teens

Rewards can be used as positive reinforcement for modifying negative behaviors. Rewards that are selected by the child are usually the most powerful. Also, a variety of reward possibilities helps to keep a child motivated over a long period of time. Rewards can be privileges, things or activities with parents. Be sure rewards don't become a substitute for words of praise and encouragement; rewards are most meaningful when given along with positive words and touch from parents. Check out these suggestions your child will love!

Home Reward Possibilities for Preschoolers

- Going to the park
- Listening to a bedtime story
- Playing with friends
- Playing on a swing set
- Spending the night with friends or grandparents
- Playing games
- Going out for ice cream
- Finger painting
- Computer time
- Staying up an hour later

Home Reward Possibilities for Elementary School Children

- Taking time off from chores
- Going to a ball game
- Camping in the backyard
- Ordering pizza
- Choosing a special breakfast
- Eating out
- Planning a day's activities
- Sleeping in a different place in the house
- Taking a trip to the park
- Selecting something special for dinner

Home Reward Possibilities for Teenagers

- Having dating privileges
- Having friends over
- Taking dancing or music lessons
- Making a trip alone
- Taking the car to school for a day
- Having car privileges
- Getting to stay out late
- Getting to sleep in late on the weekend
- Going to a concert with friends
- Having their own cell phone

Words of Encouragement and Praise

Children thrive on positive attention. Children need to feel loved and appreciated. Most parents find that it is easier to provide negative feedback rather than positive feedback. By selecting and using some of the phrases below on a daily basis with your child, you will find that he will start paying more attention to you and will try harder to please.

Yes   Good   Fine   Very good   Very fine   Excellent Marvelous At-a-boy Right

That's right   Correct Wonderful   I like the way you do that   I'm pleased with (proud of) you

That's good   Wow   Oh boy   Very nice   Good work   Great going   Good for you   That's the way

Much better   O.K.   You're doing better   That's perfect Good idea What a cleaver idea That's it

Good job   Great job controlling yourself   I like the way you _____

I noticed that you _____   Keep it up   I had fun _____ with you

You are improving at _____ more and more   You showed a lot of responsibility when you_____

Way to go   I appreciate the way you _____   You are great at that   You're the best

Good remembering   That's beautiful I like your_____

I like the way you _____ without having to be asked (reminded)

I'm sure glad you are my son/daughter   Now you've got it   I love you

<u>**You can SHOW them how you feel as well as tell them**</u>:

Smile   Nod   Part on shoulder, head, knee Wink

Signal or gesture to signify approval: High five   Touch cheek Tickle   Laugh (with, not at)

Pat on the back Hug

SECTION 3 –
Healthy Living

Healthy Living can be achieved in a well-balanced family by developing a family agreement on screen time and phone time, committing to family mealtime, and working together as a team to promote personal fitness and a healthy lifestyle. This includes getting plenty of sleep and eating nutritiously and responsibly.

Chapter 13: Family Fitness

Chapter 14: Family Mealtime

Chapter 15: The Importance of a Good Night's Sleep

CHAPTER 13

Family Fitness

OBESITY IS AN EPIDEMIC in our world today. It's not just eating more fattening foods, but the lack of activity that is contributing to the problem. You can help turn things around one day at a time by embracing a family fitness routine. If you want to get your family active but don't know how, here are some ideas you may find useful to encourage more physical activity for all family members.

Tips to Make Fitness Fun and Easy

Not everyone enjoys exercise. Doing it alone can be a chore, but when you work out with someone else, such as a family member, it can become a friendly competition that benefits all involved. Here are some easy tips you can try:

Talk to Your Family. We all could be a little more active each day. Encourage your family by telling them that you're doing it together. That way, if one person in particular needs to lose weight, they don't feel singled out. Everyone works together.

Have Fun. Especially for kids, an activity that is fun is more likely to be repeated day after day. They may even remind you about it if you forget.

Make Fitness More Accessible. It can be a hassle driving to the gym if it's not close and coordinating everyone's schedules could be a nightmare. Buy inexpensive exercise equipment to keep at home for days when you can't make it to the gym. Try DVDs, exercise bands, free weights or bicycles.

Take a Class Together. The best thing about classes is that everyone is looking at the instructor, not at you. Zumba is a hot dance exercise craze that is a great calorie burner for men and women, young and old.

Do Something Every Day. There is nothing like consistency to bring about change. Plan to do something together each day, even if only one or two can participate. Eventually, everyone will be able to get on board.

Buy Sporting Equipment. If you shop around, you should be able to find items at a reasonable price so that physical activity is only a few feet away at any given time.

Prepare the Backyard for Fun. Anytime you want to have a friendly competition, you can go outside. Keep the yard set up with a volleyball net, basketball hoop, or bases for kickball or Whiffle Ball.

Put on Some Tunes. When was the last time you and your kids danced together? If you're like most parents, you might be too busy with homework, PTA meetings, and after-school activities to hang out and dance, but it's time to start getting active. On the weekend, turn on the radio or play some of your favorite songs and dance around the house with your kids. Consider setting a timer, so you dance for at least half an hour. Don't worry about looking silly! If you're dancing for fitness, it's okay to look a little ridiculous if you work up a sweat and have a good time with your family.

Take a Walk. Walking is one of the best ways to lose weight and build your endurance. You don't need a treadmill to be able to walk. Instead, grab your family, load up the stroller and head out to explore your neighborhood. One of the best ways to enjoy walking with your family is to turn exercising into a game. Consider playing Pokémon Go and catching Pokémon in your neighborhood. You could also download a pedometer app on your phone to track how far you walk. Another option is to come up with a scavenger hunt for your kids. This doesn't have to be anything fancy. Make a list of several things you can look for on your walk. For example, you could try to find a blue house, a big leaf, a small bug, and a red car. You could make it a routine to go on a walk before or after dinner.

Exergaming. According to the American Academy of Pediatrics and the American Council on Exercise, the use of video games that engage the player in movement by playing games such as bowling, tennis or following exercise routines can be a safe and effective tool for maintaining or improving cardiovascular fitness. Depending on the games/exercises and the time spent, you can burn off some serious calories. Research has also found that these games help children develop balance and motor skills. The three most-used systems are:

- **Kinect for Xbox One.** With multiplayer and single-player games that include boxing, volleyball, Kung Fu, track and field, soccer and more, the Kinect for Xbox One is hands-free–using a sensor in the game console to track movement, then translate it into game play.

- **PlayStation Move.** Employing a camera and a motion controller remote, this gaming console offers exercise game titles for single and multi-player play, including beach volleyball, disc golf, archery, dance, table tennis, kickboxing and more.

- **Nintendo Wii Fit.** Featuring multiplayer and single-player games, including skateboarding, Hula, Kung Fu, skiing, dance games and more, the Wii Fit uses a balance board and remote, both of which translate real-life movement into game play.

TV Commercial Breaks. Turn television commercial breaks into exercise breaks. Get up off the couch and do some running in place, jumping jacks, push-ups or some other brief exercise.

Encourage Outdoor Activities. Encourage your children to ride bikes, skateboard, go swimming or participate in other outdoor activities.

Family Outings. Go to the park and let the kids play on the equipment. Go for a hike. Rent bikes or a rowboat. Go bowling or miniature golfing. Go to the beach, lake or a community pool.

Fitness for a Cause. Communities often have walking or running events to raise money for a charity. This is the perfect opportunity for a family activity, or even as a way to spend some one-on-one time with a child. Other possibilities are community or environmental clean-up events and projects such as Habitat for Humanity.

Household Chores. Work around the house or the yard can provide excellent opportunities for physical activity.

Be a role model. Kids are more apt to follow what they see. If you, as a parent, are active, they will try to follow suit. You can turn things around in your family. It's never too late to get healthier and more active. No matter how you and your family decide to get fit, remember, the important thing is spending time together in healthy ways. While working out together might be tough at first, you'll soon find that you're not only growing closer as a family, but you're growing healthier as well.

At your family meetings, each member can set personal fitness goals, such as how far they plan to walk each day, and how much time they will spend on fitness activities. Each family member should keep track of their progress and share their results with the rest of the family. Make time to celebrate any milestones or accomplishments.

Some children may be hesitant to participate in organized sports. This may be due to lack of self-confidence, difficulty with motor coordination, social anxiety, immature social skills or they have competing interests in other types of activities such as music, art, reading, or hobbies. Kids shouldn't view exercise as a punishment. Forcing a child to exercise or play a sport will not be productive. You can encourage your child to go out and ride their bike before doing homework. Find age-appropriate activities they may feel more comfortable doing, such as running, swimming, yoga, Karate, jumping rope or learning to play tennis or golf. Just going for a walk is good exercise. What about going for a "hike" in a nearby park?

Some kids lack confidence in their skills, though they may want to play in a particular team sport. You could work with them to develop skills such as throwing and catching a ball, shooting hoops, or hitting a ball with a bat. Finding a coach to work with them individually or enrolling them in a class through your local recreational and parks program might also work. Most important, is letting your children know you love them and are proud of them just the way they are—point out some of their talents, skills, and personal qualities.

You could see if one of your child's friends is interested in learning a sport or other physical activity and encourage your child to participate along with them. Be patient and suggest that your child try several sports activities to find one that works for them. If they join for a while and then want to quit, you may first try to understand his or her reason for quitting and provide encouragement. However, if they insist, let them stop and wait a bit and look for another way for them to engage in physical activity on a regular basis.

CHAPTER 14
Family Mealtime

MANY FAMILIES HAVE GOTTEN away from the tradition of sitting down together for breakfast in the morning and dinner in the evening. It's easy to see why if you look at all the events and errands that take place on any given day. Kids have after-school activities, dental appointments, and doctor visits. Parents, on the other hand, are usually dropping the kids off somewhere either before or after work and running errands. It isn't always an easy task to arrange for a meal when everyone isn't at home at the same time.

Recent studies have shown that not only do children like to sit down at the dinner table and eat a meal with their parents, but they are more likely to eat a well-balanced, nutritious meal when they do. However, with the hectic lives we seem to lead these days, getting the family all together in the same place at the same time can be a difficult task. With a few simple ideas and some planning, mealtime can be enjoyable and treasured family time.

Some Great Reasons for Family Meal Time

Better Nutrition and Health. According to a study published in 2011 in the Journal of the American Academy of Pediatrics, children are less likely to develop bad eating habits, or worse yet, eating disorders, if they have the opportunity to sit down and enjoy a traditional family meal setting every day. In fact, the same study also suggests that children who eat with their families are more likely to develop good eating habits, including choosing healthier foods over unhealthy ones.

Of course, it's important to realize the critical role parents play, mainly because most children learn by example. If parents fail to serve nutritional meals during family mealtimes, it will become more difficult for their children to develop good eating habits. On the other hand, parents who continually emphasize healthy choices, such as fresh vegetables and fruits, lean meats, and whole grains are giving their child an opportunity to learn how to eat healthily.

Interpersonal Bonding. Thanks to technology, parents today might never have an actual conversation with their kids if they didn't need to drive them to school or a friend's house. Everyone is texting instead of talking. While this might be an exaggeration, it's true to a certain extent. Just look around you. How many people are on their phones right now?

Despite the ease with which many people become more comfortable talking to their friends and family members via email and texting, one-on-one communication in person is vital. Even though texting shortcuts such as "LOL" and "OMG" might regularly appear in your child's messages, does this tell you anything about your kid? Do you know for a fact that your child is happy? Would you be able to recognize if your child was hiding behind the screen because he didn't want you to see how unhappy he is?

Conversation during family meals has also been found by researchers to promote language development. Through discussions, parents can interject new words to build vocabulary. By sharing what happened during the day, children develop their skill at using narratives to share experiences. By asking questions, parents can help improve their child's ability to provide a more thorough description. You can teach and reinforce the foundation of any narrative: "who, what, where, when and why." Further questions can encourage your kids to share how they feel about the event and what it may have caused them to think about as well.

Sharing your own stories also provides a model for younger children to learn how to add more details and a logical flow to their narrative. Adding your thoughts and feelings encourages more open communication.

Discussing books read by parents and kids fosters the development of literacy while encouraging continued reading. Discussion of the content, regardless of whether it's fiction or nonfiction, improves comprehension. It could also serve as a springboard for further reading on a topic, further reading by a fiction writer or the discovery of other authors they may find entertaining. Following up on reading could also lead to thinking about activities that promote curiosity and learning. Reading a book on science could lead to going to a museum or getting a science kit. Reading about a musician or artist might develop into an interest to try out music or art lessons.

Discussion about current events can open opportunities for parents to impart values. It can also be used to teach critical thinking skills. Moreover, it provides a chance to help kids learn to distinguish between reliable and unreliable sources of information.

Family mealtimes are excellent opportunities for bonding. They provide a chance not only to share the day's events but also to get to know each other a little better. Even without a food fight, you're more likely to discover what makes your child laugh or cry over a family meal than you are through a short text message. This is especially true if you had to learn how to decipher the text before you even knew what it meant.

One tradition some families use to encourage sharing their day with others at the dinner table is called "Thorns & Roses." As you go around to all family members at the table, each person shares one "Thorn" or something not-so-good that happened to them that day, and one "Rose," which is something good that happened to them that day.

Sometimes during dinner, a family member may bring up a problem during a discussion. If it's personal and related to the individual, you might respond by saying, "I understand why that's bothering you. Why don't we talk about that after dinner privately?" If the problem is more family related you might say, "That sounds like something we should spend some time problem-solving. Why don't we discuss that at our next family meeting?" The concept is to keep the focus of family meals on sharing and interacting rather than problem-solving.

How to Make Family Meal Time Enjoyable for All

Assign each person in the family a task to help prepare the meals. There's no reason why only one family member should have to do all the cooking if others can pitch in. You might also find that some of the best conversations happen as you're preparing a meal together. Find tasks for even the youngest members of the family.

Preparing and serving your meals at the same time each day will promote a sense of routine in your home. Your family will come to know that if it's close to 5:30 p.m., they need to get home or risk missing dinner. Having meals around the same time each day also discourages snacking between meals.

Preparing and sharing meals is also an excellent way to influence what your children eat. Talk about why certain foods are healthy and why other options aren't. Talk about how food provides nourishment and why it's important to refrain from eating too many refined and sweet foods.

Children who share meals with their family have been shown to do better in school. Part of the reason is that the food they eat is more nutritious than what can get at any fast food drive-thru. Having parents who ask about what's going on at school also encourages them to do better and handle problems that arise there in an appropriate manner.

You may also be surprised to know that sharing meals as a family can cut down on the chances that your child will become involved with drugs or alcohol. When teens get involved in things they shouldn't, it's often because they're trying to get their parents' attention. Children who eat meals with their family already have the attention they desire. Who knew sharing meals could be so important? By eating together regularly, you can help your child excel in school, keep them off drugs, and stay connected with them.

Does having a family meal mean you must cook something out of the ordinary? Absolutely not! As long as you're together around a table sharing a meal, you can be eating takeout, and the benefits will be the same. If you choose to have pizza delivered, order something without all kinds of meat and go with veggies instead. Or better yet, make a healthy pizza at home.

Keep in mind—your kids will probably require snacks in the afternoon. Rather than ban them altogether, stock up on healthy foods such as fruits and vegetables. Greek yogurt, popcorn, and wheat crackers with cheese are other snacks you can feel good about having in your home.

Give your teen some say about what you eat as a family. Of course, you'll want to quell their desire for nothing but junk food, but if they have more input into what you eat, they may be less likely to fight you. Teach your kids how to make a meal plan and shop for groceries to help prepare them for when it's time to leave home.

Finally, as a means to encourage your kids to make the right food choices, explain to them the benefits of choosing foods carefully. Fruits, veggies, whole grains, nuts, and lean proteins will provide teens with the nutrients they need to be their best. Fast and fried foods may taste good, but they lead to sluggishness and ill health.

How to Make Your Life Easier with Meal Plans

A menu plan begets a focused grocery shopping list. How many times have you gone to the store only to realize once you get home that you've forgotten to buy one or two essential items? Keep a pad and pen nearby and write down ingredients for each planned meal. You can also keep track of what you need in your smartphone with the notebook function or with a grocery app like Grocery IQ (available for iOS and Android). A menu plan allows you to save time in the kitchen. Knowing that you have everything you need because you've kept track of it means no last-minute runs to the store or awkward substitutions.

You can make a menu plan for one week, two weeks, or if you're feeling highly organized, you can plan out one month in advance. Keep each week's menu plan in a journal, file, or your phone or computer. Make notes about which meals your family likes and dislikes, and any modifications that might make the meal better. Be creative and don't be afraid to experiment with recipes! You can also make "snack plans." Come up with a healthy after-school snack for each school day of the week.

How to Make a Meal Plan

- Make a list of all the dishes your family enjoys. This can be done at the family meeting.

- Save dishes that take longer than 30 minutes to prepare (not counting cooking time), for days when you have more time.

- Put each main dish into categories such as Mexican, Italian, sandwiches, soups, salads, casseroles, lunch-for-dinner, breakfast-for-dinner, etc.

- Leftovers are your best friend. Many meals still taste great when reheated, and eating leftovers saves time and money.

- Make the quickest and easiest meals on the busiest nights.

- Create a routine with your weekly meal schedule, e.g., Taco Tuesdays, Italian on Mondays, make-your-own sandwiches on Fridays. Instilling tradition in your kids' lives, even in the smallest of ways, will help your family stay connected.

- After you've chosen your meal categories, it's time to look through your cupboards to see which ingredients you already have and which ingredients you need to purchase. Take your time with this.

Organize your pantry, throw out old food, and make lists of what you already have.

- Be flexible. Plans change, people stop by, meetings pop up and sometimes you just feel like being waited on at a restaurant. By having a meal plan, you can choose to switch meals from one day to another and still know you have everything you need.

- Before you know it, you'll practically have your own personalized family cookbook with solid go-to recipes.

Here are some helpful resources for meal plans:

eMeals.com is a great low-cost way to get weekly meal plans. You select recipes you want for the week, and their app will create the shopping list for you. All you have to do is cook the meal. You can select meals at your family meeting. You can teach older kids how to follow the recipes and prepare the meals.

You can get free information on meal planning for families on a budget from the US Department of Agriculture using these web links:

[cnpp.usda.gov/sites/default/files/usda_food_plans_cost_of_food/ FoodPlansRecipeBook.pdf]

[nutrition.gov/subject/shopping-cooking-meal-planning/ food-shopping-and-meal-planning]

CHAPTER 15

The Importance of a Good Night's Sleep

SLEEP IS ESSENTIAL TO both physical and mental health. Numerous research studies published in the last few years have documented the fact that a sizeable number of children, teens, and adults are not getting the recommended amount of sleep. In 2014, the Center for Disease Control reported that 33% of adults are not getting sufficient sleep. Also, in 2014, the results of a poll conducted by the National Sleep Foundation found that most parents reported that their children were getting fewer hours of sleep than recommended for the child's age. And according to a study published by the American Academy of Pediatrics in 2018, only 8% of US teens get the number of hours of sleep recommended for that age group.

Sleep experts state the increase in lack of sufficient sleep across all age groups is attributable to lifestyle changes occurring over the last ten years. One factor mentioned in these studies is increased stress for many in our society, and it cuts across all age groups. Adults are spending more hours working, and children and teens are spending more time with homework and extracurricular activities.

The second major factor is increased screen time on multiple digital devices. In addition to the increase in the amount of time spent on these devices, many Americans are using them right up until they go to bed, and quite a few continue to use them even after they get in bed. Teens I've seen in my practice tell me they lie in bed and text or chat for hours. Some kids share they get under the covers and play games on their phone or tablet. I know adults who lie in bed texting, reading and responding to emails after they go to bed.

The connection with the use of these devices within an hour of bedtime and difficulty falling asleep is the blue light emitted from all screens, including TVs, computers, phones, tablets, and video games. This light tricks the brain into thinking it is still daytime, and therefore the brain suppresses the release of melatonin, a hormone that induces sleep. Because of this phenomenon, sleep experts recommend turning off digital devices at least 30 minutes to one hour before bedtime.

Lack of appropriate amounts of sleep has profound effects on physical and mental health. Impairment in attention, concentration, working memory, and other executive functions lowers work performance for adults and academic achievement for children and adolescents. Poor sleep is associated with higher rates of hypertension, diabetes, obesity, and depression. Also, lack of appropriate sleep time increases the chance of causing an automobile accident due to falling asleep at the wheel. Over 55% of these accidents involve a driver under age 25.

Given that lack of sleep can affect all members of the family, it makes sense for improving sleep to become a family priority with a family-oriented approach. Children and teens who observe parents following the same rules for good rest are more likely to follow the rules without too much protest.

Following are the recommended hours of sleep from the National Sleep Foundation for children and adults:

Age Range	Recommended Hours of Sleep
3-5	10-13 hours per day, including naps
6-13	9-11 hours per day
14-17	8-10 hours per day
Adults	7-9 hours per day

Cutting back on screen time should be goal number one. This means that all electronics are shut down 30 minutes to 1 hour before bedtime. Studies indicate that over 70% of kids and teens have at least one screen device in their bedroom. Parents should share information with kids on how the blue light affects our ability to get to sleep. Many sleep advocates recommend that children and teens not have any electronic screen devices in their rooms, including TVs, computers, tablets, video games, and phones. An old-fashioned alarm clock can serve as a wake-up signal for those who need one rather than a smartphone.

Older kids can learn how to schedule their homework, so assignments requiring a device with a screen are completed first. Also, teach kids how to do their homework in chunks of about 45 minutes with a 10-minute break in between. During the afternoon or early evening (an hour before bedtime), a light exercise break is a great use of some of the break times. It re-energizes the brain.

Parents and kids should agree on a bedtime that will allow them to get the recommended hours of sleep based on their age. Parents should set an appropriate bedtime for themselves and stick to it as well.

Where we sleep is important. If possible, bedrooms should exist primarily for sleeping. For adults, the only use of the bedroom other than sleeping should be for sex. This will help your brain to associate this location with going to sleep. If needed, purchase an alarm clock. If you or your kids wake up and start staring at the clock worrying about how long you've been awake, turn it away from you. An iPod or another device without a screen for listening to music should be okay.

In addition to the above, bedrooms should be cozy and quiet. A comfortable bed and bedding is a must. The temperature should be on the cool side (60-67 degrees). Low levels of sound in the room are important (use earplugs or a white noise machine if needed). People sleep better in a cooler environment. There should be as little light as possible in the room. If your child is afraid of the dark, a small dimly lit night light should work well. Younger kids may be comforted by having a doll, plush toy or blanket with which to snuggle.

Here are a few tips for getting a good night's sleep, also known as sleep hygiene:

- For teens and adults, limit naps to once per day, for 30 minutes.

- Avoid stimulants such as caffeine or nicotine close to bedtime. Some recommend having none of these beyond the early afternoon. Also, avoid snacks such as chips, chocolate, and soft drinks in the evening.

- Avoid heavy meals when possible.

- Keep a regular bedtime and wakeup time.

- Get exercise during the day. Light exercise such as stretching is okay before bed, but vigorous exercise should be avoided at least one hour before bed time.

- Encourage kids to try to exercise in the morning. Research shows that children who engage in 20 to 30 minutes of exercise in the morning do much better academically during the school day than those who don't.

- Be sure to get adequate exposure to light during the day. Lack of light exposure during the day can interrupt the sleep/wake cycle. Also, more children, teens and adults have low Vitamin D levels due to lack of exposure to daylight.

- Help control nightmares by being mindful of what you and your kids watch on TV before going to bed.

- Have a regular, relaxing routine before going to bed, such as taking a warm shower or bath, reading a book, listening to relaxing music or light stretching. For children, a nighttime routine could include a parent reading to the child for 10 to 20 minutes. For teens, listening to an audiobook might work.

When everyone in the family has their own bed time and sticks to it, everyone benefits. If you or your child have difficulty falling asleep, frequently have restless sleep, or feel tired during the day (even though you've gotten the recommended amount of sleep), you should discuss this with your physician. Don't try over-the-counter medication, herbs or other sleep aids without talking to your physician first.

If you or your child wake up and can't go back to sleep, get up for 20 minutes and read or listen to soft music, and then go back to bed. If you get up again, read a boring book such as a textbook. Another trick that helps people go to sleep or get back to sleep is to take a quick "mental vacation." Start by taking ten deep breaths. Then close your eyes and imagine you're at a favorite place like the beach or a hiking trail. Try to be fully involved by seeing everything there is to see, hearing everything there is to hear, feeling anything there is to feel such as the warmth of the sun or a cool breeze and doing anything you like to do while you're in that spot.

If a child wakes up, don't let them stay in your room. Instead, bring them back to their room. You could read a short story and then tuck them in. If they continue to want to come to your bedroom, get a chair and bring it to your child's room and sit until they fall asleep. This will help them associate falling asleep and getting up in the morning in their own bedroom.

It's good to put kids to bed when they're drowsy but awake. Allowing them to sleep in places other than their bed teaches them to fall asleep in other areas instead of their own bed. If you and your family follow these simple suggestions for good sleep hygiene, you will all start getting the sleep you need to stay healthy, happy, and productive.

Section 3 – Family Fitness - Summary

Ideas & Recommendations for Increasing Fitness in Your Family

Suggestions for Improving Your Family's Lifestyle and Promoting Health and Wellbeing for All Family Members:

1. During a family meeting, discuss and decide on a family and individual approach for the use of electronics in the home.

   a. Implement the family docking station (See Chapter 17).

   b. Use the Media and Children Communication Tool Kit from the American Academy of Pediatrics to help each family member develop a Media Use Plan.

   c. Have all family members sign and commit to their pledge as part of the Family Contract for Online Safety available from *SafeKids.com.*

2. Discuss the concept of family mealtime at a family meeting. Decide how you can implement it in your home.

   a. Agree to a schedule.

   b. Implement suggestions for communication during meals.

   c. Develop ideas for family meals. See the resources for Chapter 14 for help with this project. Also consider the Eat Sheet and Family Meal Planner as tools to help.

   d. Discuss progress at family meetings.

3. At a family meeting, discuss individual and family goals for increasing exercise.

   a. Develop individual goals. The Exercise Apple, Exercise List and Two-Week Exercise Log may be useful tools.

   b. Plan family exercise activities. Some should include the entire family while others might be for 1:1 time with a parent and an individual child.

    c.   See resources for Chapter 13 for additional suggestions and tools.

4. Discuss the importance of sleep as a family. Encourage a discussion about sleep between your kids and their primary care physician. The Bedtime Routine chart may help with implementing the suggestions in Chapter 15 and the additional resources for Chapter 15.

Tools for Success: Healthy Living

Exercise Activity Ideas: This is a simple suggestion list that may help your kids find activities they would like to try.

Personal Monthly Exercise Log: This is a great way for all members of the family to keep track of their exercise activities. The monthly total can be used in family challenge records.

Family Exercise Challenge – Record of Success: The idea here is for each family member to set a goal for how much time they want to spend exercising and share their progress with the rest of the family. You can share at family meetings and praise successes and cheer each other on.

Family Meal Planner: A simple way to build a weekly meal plan and keep track of grocery needs to make the meals.

Bedtime Routine: This provides a tool to help children be ready for bed on time and to follow good sleep preparation steps.

- Enter agreed upon time to start unwinding activities (at least one-half hour before bedtime).

- List unwinding time such as read a book, listen to music, take a warm bath, etc. It could be just one. (For young children, you can paste or draw a picture as a cue).

- Use the same instructions for Ready of Bed. Activities may include brush teeth, put on pajamas, etc.

- Finally, In Bed Time should be indicated. Once your child is in bed, you may still want to do a short routine of reading a short story, saying prayers, etc.

- Use this chart for about 4 weeks (Check off when time is met, and activities are completed).

Please be sure to visit parentingtoday.com/tools for PDF versions of the charts provided at the end of each section as well as additional resources, including updates, classes, and forums for parents.

Exercise Activity Ideas
Things I Can Do to Keep Busy and Fit

Go for a walk	Practice karate moves
Go running	Do some jumping jacks
Ride my skateboard	Do some push-ups
Ski	Do some sit-ups
Fly a kite	Work in the garden
Ride my bike	Rake leaves
Run through the sprinklers	Shovel snow
Jump rope	Sweep the sidewalk
Throw a Frisbee	Mow the lawn
Go for a hike	Vacuum
Go Rollerblading	Play golf or miniature golf
Walk the dog	Go bowling
Ride my scooter	Work out at the gym or Y
Play at the park	Gymnastics
Go swimming	Play hopscotch
Go ice skating	Play Wii Fit Games
Dance	Do Wii Fit Exercise Routines
Yoga	Shoot Hoops

Personal Monthly Exercise Log

Name: _____ Month: _____

Day	Date	Activity	Time Spent	Checked
Monday				
Tuesday				
Wednesday				
Thursday				
Friday				
Saturday				
Sunday				
		Total Exercise Time For The Week:		

Day	Date	Activity	Time Spent	Checked
Monday				
Tuesday				
Wednesday				
Thursday				
Friday				
Saturday				
Sunday				
		Total Exercise Time for The Week:		

Day	Date	Activity	Time Spent	Checked
Monday				
Tuesday				
Wednesday				
Thursday				
Friday				
Saturday				
Sunday				
		Total Exercise Time for The Week:		

Day	Date	Activity	Time Spent	Checked
Monday				
Tuesday				
Wednesday				
Thursday				
Friday				
Saturday				
Sunday				
		Total Exercise Time for The Week:		
		Total Exercise Time for The Month:		

Family Exercise Challenge – Record of Success

Month													
Team Member													
Total Time													
Goal													
+/- Goal													
Team Member													
Total Time													
Goal													
+/- Goal													
Team Member													
Total Time													
Goal													
+/- Goal													
Team Member													
Total Time													
Goal													
+/- Goal													
Team Member													
Total Time													
Goal													
+/- Goal													
Team Member													
Total Time													
Goal													
+/- Goal													

Family Meal Planner

Meal Plans	Shopping List
Monday	
Tuesday	
Wednesday	
Thursday	
Friday	
Saturday	
Sunday	

Bedtime Routine Chart

Name: _____

	Mon	Tue	Wed	Thr	Fri	Sat	Sun
Unwind Time:							
Unwind Activities:							
1.							
2.							
3.							
Ready for Bed Time:							
Ready for Bed Activities:							
1.							
2.							
3.							
In Bed Time:							

SECTION 4 –
Organization

Organization happens when a family works together to develop a plan to achieve their goals. For it to be effective, all members of the family need to be heard, and the plan should be developed collaboratively with the acknowledgement that the adults must have the final say.

Chapter 16: Family Meetings

Chapter 17: Managing Screen Time and Cyber Safety Measures

Chapter 18: Getting Your Family Organized & Working Together

Chapter 19: Home / School Issues

CHAPTER 16
Family Meetings

HOLDING REGULAR FAMILY MEETINGS is the key to using all the suggestions in this book to develop a well-balanced family. This concept may sound strange to many of you. Most families don't hold regular meetings—they usually handle issues as they come up. Some may meet to plan a trip or another project, but discussing day-to-day issues are generally impromptu and can be heated as well as consisting of mostly one-way communication.

Family meetings should occur weekly on a day and time that works well for all family members. Parents are encouraged to meet and come up with some possibilities, and then discuss the concept with each child individually as well as listen to any ideas they might have. For some, a Friday evening after dinner, maybe over a special dessert, would work. The meetings don't have to be long—20 minutes or so should work. When meeting with each child, parents should let them know that the purpose of the meetings is for them to share ideas for fun activities and discuss how the family can run smoothly for everyone.

At the meetings, the parents serve as facilitators and should encourage their children to share their thoughts and feelings openly. To be sure that only one family member shares at a time, an object such as a ball or a stuffed animal may be selected as the family totem and should be passed from one to the other when requested. The person holding the totem is the only one who has the floor.

Family meetings are an excellent time to teach and reinforce some key skills and attitudes, such as brainstorming, looking at the pros and cons of a dilemma or proposed action, accepting and listening to the thoughts and opinions of others without judging, patient listening, and providing encouragement and support to others. *Our Family Meeting Book* by Elaine Hightower and Betsy Riley provide family meeting agendas you could employ as you see as being pertinent to personal or family issues or skills you think would be valuable for your children. Topics include sharing, teamwork and cooperation, foul language and family values, manners, negotiation, and resolving conflicts.

Everyone needs to understand that the meeting should be friendly and free of criticism. For instance, there is no such thing as a bad idea. It should be made clear that the parents have the final say on any decision making. You can explain that this is no different from meetings that adults hold at work where the boss may have the final say.

The primary purpose of the meeting is to plan family activities and solve problems related to living together in harmony, as well as supporting each other on both individual and shared goals. Each meeting should have an agenda, created at the previous meeting, with input from all. Someone may wish to volunteer to take informal minutes at each meeting. You should also have a copy of the family calendar to update as the result of decisions made at the meeting. Other items to have at the meeting, if you have them, would be a chore chart and individual or family goal charts.

The basic steps of brainstorming are the following:

1. Identify and describe the problem using the "5 W's" (Who, What, Where, When and Why).

2. Encourage everyone to give suggests for solving the problem. It's probably a good idea to write them down as they're given. At this stage in the process, all ideas are possibly good ideas.

3. Take each solution and look at the pros and cons. Encourage open and free discussion. Everybody has an opinion and they should be heard.

4. The family should look at all of the ideas and the pros and cons of each and come to a consensus on which idea or a combination of ideas that seem feasible should be tried out.

5. Come up with a plan for giving the idea a try and a set of criteria to evaluate its effectiveness.

6. Set a timeline for implementing the idea and when to evaluate its success with the understanding that it might need to be revised or replaced if it doesn't pass muster.

Guidelines for Running Family Meetings

- Family meetings should include all members of the family, including parents, children and anyone else living in the home, such as grandparents or others.

- Make the first meeting a short one to agree on a regular time for the weekly meeting.

- One family member should serve as the moderator and another should serve as a secretary to take notes and keep the agenda.

- Some families find it beneficial to make a family meeting binder that holds the minutes but also the family calendar, goal sheets, and activity plans.

- Keep the meetings upbeat and fun. Be sure only one person talks at a time.

- Here are some suggestions for a family meeting agenda. Most likely only a few will be discussed at a given meeting:

  * Share compliments reflecting the past week.

  * Share any apologies related to the past week.

- Review the "I Can Pledge" and the elements of HOMES.

- Come up with family or personal affirmations for the week.

- Review the agenda.

- Review the minutes from the last meeting. Identify goals or tasks that need continued work and/or discussion.

- Discuss progress towards fitness goals.

- Discuss upcoming family activities such as outings, movie night, game night, etc.

- Discuss the meal plans as needed.

- Review responsibilities including the chore chart, etc.

- Discuss financial issues such as allowances and the family budget as needed.

- Discuss any problem that requires the attention of the entire family.

- End with a fun activity.

CHAPTER 17

Managing Screen Time and Cyber Safety Measures

Issues to Consider When Monitoring Your Family's Screen Time

KIDS TODAY SPEND MUCH of their time in front of a screen, be it a TV, computer, smartphone or tablet. Technology has many positive uses and can provide helpful information, entertainment and even enhance social engagement but like anything else, there needs to be a balance in how much time is spent using electronics.

Social Interaction. It is not uncommon for a growing number of kids and teens to spend most or sometimes all of their interaction with others through texting, calling, gaming, and social media. Personal interactions with others are limited, and social and conversational skills are affected. Kids need contact with other kids to develop healthy relationships with each other.

Physical Health. Too much time sitting promotes poor eating habits and lack of physical exercise. Being too focused on a video game or computer activity interferes with intentional, healthy eating. A child is more likely to snack on foods that aren't nutritious.

Learning. Studies have shown that children who spend more than two hours a day in front of the TV or another device have a more limited vocabulary, have homework problems, and are more at risk for attention deficit disorder. Other research indicates that reading is a more powerful learning tool than digital devices including the computer.

Sleep Problems. Many kids take their phones or computers to bed with them. The hours before bedtime can make the difference between a good night's sleep and interrupted sleep. The lights from these devices trick the brain into thinking it is daylight, as well as cause over-stimulation.

Behavioral Problems. A recent study published in *Pediatrics* indicates that children who watch television or play computer games for more than two hours a day have a higher risk for psychological problems. This study examined over 1,000 children between 10 and 11 years of age and found that violent movies or video games can contribute to aggressive behaviors and fights with family and friends.

Addiction. The habitual use of electronics can not only impede a healthy lifestyle, but it can also become an obsession. Try removing the screens, and you might see agitation, restlessness, and a striking change in attitude. Some research indicates that as many as 25% of children and teens may be addicted to screen use (Internet, video games, social media, or television). Certain activities involving screen activity can produce the release of neurotransmitters in the pleasure center of the brain. This is also stimulated by other pleasurable activities and interactions with others, as well certain foods and substances. Many video games are programmed to provide a reward (reaching a new level, awarding points, or getting a new tool or weapon) every 20 minutes. This results in sustained use of the game.

A study published by the University of Michigan in 2017 concluded that screen addiction is not necessarily related to the amount of time a child spends using digital media but how dependent they are on screen time. Here are the signs they identified as indicators of possible screen addiction:

- **Unsuccessful Control.** A child has difficulty stopping and refraining from screen use and accepting parental imposed/suggested limits.

- **Lack of Interest in Other Activities.** All of a sudden, your child who loved to read books or play sports says they're boring, and they don't want to spend time on them anymore.

- **Preoccupies Their Thoughts.** All they can talk about is their favorite video game, app on their tablet, or the videos they watch on *YouTube*.

- **Interferes with Socializing.** They stop playing with friends and/or don't want to join in family activities, or they drop out of outside activities.

- **Causes Major Family Problems.** Arguments arise over screen use. They become argumentative and/or aggressive when you discuss the issue or set limits.

- **Withdrawal Symptoms.** When it is time to put screen devices down to do homework, go to bed, engage in a family activity, or spend one-on-one time with a parent, they become frustrated and upset.

- **Increasing Tolerance.** The amount of time they spend on a given screen activity starts to increase or they seem like they just can't get enough.

- **Deception.** They start sneaking their phone or tablet into the bedroom or outside. They hide under their covers at night using the device.

- **Mood Boost.** When your child is upset about something, they turn to the screen to feel better.

If you notice any of these signs, you should discuss your observations with your child's primary care physician. Pediatric and Family Practice physicians are now receiving training and information on this topic and can be a great resource. A school counselor or school psychologist may also be a valuable resource. *Reset Your Child's Brain: A Four-Week Plan to End Meltdowns, Raise*

Grades, and Boost Social Skills by Reversing the Effects of Electronic Screen-Time by Victoria L. Dunckley MD, Coleen Marlo, et al. published on May 8, 2018, is a recommended resource for help for this problem. If you don't find this helpful, you may need a referral to a child and adolescent mental health specialist (child psychologist or licensed clinical social worker specializing in children).

A parent has the responsibility of setting limits and monitoring their child's overall electronic activity. Sit down and discuss with your child how the screens should be used, for how long, and why. Open communication is the key to helping your child use their time wisely and healthily.

Seven Suggestions for Controlling & Monitoring Use of Electronic Devices:

(1) Designate areas of your home that should be screen-free. This should include bedrooms–at least a bedtime. There should be no televisions in a bedroom for children and teens. All other electronic devices should be stored outside the bedroom before bedtime.

(2) Another area should be the dining table; not just during family meals, but for any time someone is eating there. Parents can teach their kids mindful eating. This helps reduce food consumption and improves digestion. Family mealtime should become an opportunity for positive interaction and open communication between all family members.

(3) If possible, an office/study room should be available with access to a computer, books, and other materials for work or study. A bulletin board placed on a wall could serve as a place to post homework schedules and reading logs. It is best if kids have a designated area for work as it improves concentration and task completion.

(4) Buy a docking station that is large enough to accommodate all of the family's portable devices (phones and tablets) and place it in a central location. Devices should be plugged in when entering the home and should remain there except for agreed-upon times for their use. Ideally, parents should wait to retrieve texts or phone calls until times when they're not engaged in family time. Better yet, if possible, save that activity for after the kids are in bed.

(5) Each member of the family should have a daily activity schedule that includes screen time. You can discuss this at a family meeting. At the meeting times, limits for each member of the family should be set and agreed upon. Times may vary based on the age of the child. This process may not be easy, but it's a good topic for problem-solving. You may want to spend time with each child helping them to come up with their own priorities of what shows to watch and other activities to fit within their time limit.

(6) Screens should be turned off when engaging in socialization or other activities such as completing homework. Distraction during social exchanges or multitasking is always counterproductive.

(7) Parents need to be role models. Agree to limits on your own use during family meetings and stick with them. You can use Screen Time to monitor your use and set limits.

In addition to the above, learning how to set parental controls on various devices is very important. By using these tools, you'll be able to monitor your child's usage, set time limits, and restrict their use to age-appropriate content. Below are the basic directions for Mac and Windows computers and both IOS and Android devices:

Setting Parental Controls on a Mac

You'll find Parental Controls under System Preferences. You can monitor and control the time your children spend on the Mac and the websites they visit. To set up parental controls for your children, follow these steps:

1. Turn on parental controls for each child. If you haven't added a user account for your child to your Mac, see "Add a new user" to manage with parental controls. If you've already added an account for your

child, see "Turn on parental controls" for a child with an existing account on your Mac.

2. Change the restrictions you want for each child. For example, you can decide which websites your child can visit, and how long they can use the Mac each day.

3. If you want, copy the settings for one child and use them for another child.

4. When you decide your child is ready, you can turn off parental controls for them.

For detailed instructions please use this link:

[support.apple.com/guide/mac-help/set-up-parental-controls-mtusr004/mac]

Parental Controls for Windows

If you want to manage your child's time and activities on the PC, Windows 10 includes a built-in function called "Family Safety." Setting up parental controls in prior versions of Windows was always a chore.

Unlike Windows 7, which managed your child's experience locally, this occurs through the Microsoft Accounts page. So, you'll need to ensure you have an active Internet connection to successfully configure the application of Family Safety Settings in Windows 10. Here are some of the activities you can manage:

• Family Safety will let you block an account.

• Collect and receive activity reports.

• Block and view websites your child visits on the computer.

• Review apps and games your child can access.

• Manage when they use the device.

Configure Settings: To start setting up Family Safety, head to Click Start > Settings > Accounts. Or use the keyboard shortcut Windows Key + I and select Accounts.

For complete information and directions, please use this link: [account.microsoft.com/family/]

Setting Parental Controls for iPhones. iPads, and iPods

With Content & Privacy Restrictions in Screen Time, you can block or limit specific apps and features on your child's device. You can also restrict the settings on your iPhone, iPad, or iPod touch for explicit content, purchases and downloads, and privacy. Here are the options you will have using these settings:

- Set Content & Privacy Restrictions
- Prevent explicit content and content ratings
- Prevent web content
- Prevent iTunes & App Store purchases
- Restrict Siri web search
- Allow changes to privacy settings
- Allow built-in apps and features
- Restrict Game Center
- Allow changes to other settings and features

Here are the basic directions:

1. Go to Settings and tap "Screen Time."

2. Tap "Continue," then choose "This is My iPhone" or "This is My Child's iPhone."

3. If you're the parent or guardian of your device and want to prevent another family member from changing your settings, tap "Use Screen Time Passcode" to create a passcode. Then re-enter the passcode to confirm.

4. If you're setting up Screen Time on your child's device, follow the prompts until you get to Parent Passcode and enter a passcode. Re-enter the passcode to confirm.

5. Tap "Content & Privacy Restrictions." If asked, enter your passcode, then turn on Content & Privacy.

Please follow this link for directions on how to set all of the specific features. [support.apple.com/en-us/HT201304]

Android Parental Control Set-up

1. Open the Settings menu of your device. Locate the gear icon on the home screen, notification panel, or app drawer, and tap it. This will open all the Settings menu for your device.

2. Scroll down and tap "Users." This will open a menu where you can add new users to the device.

3. Add a restricted user profile. Tap "Add user or profile" and from the options, select "Restricted profile."

4. Set up a password for the account. This is in case you don't have a password yet. To do this, select the security option you prefer (PIN, password, or pattern), then enter the PIN, password, or pattern for it.

5. Once you're done, a new screen will appear listing all the installed apps on the device. Each will have a toggle ON/OFF button adjacent to them.

6. Name the profile. Tap the three-line icon adjacent to the "New profile" option at the top of the screen. In the dialog box that appears, enter the profile name; this could be your child's name. When you're done, tap "OK."

7. Select apps to enable for the profile. You can now choose the apps that the profile user will have access to. For instance, if you want your child to have access to only his/her games, then choose only the game apps. To select apps, tap the toggle button next to the app to ON. Leave those apps that you don't want your child to access to OFF.

8. Use the new restricted profile. Exit the Settings menu and lock the screen. Activate the screen by pressing the Home button of the device. You will now be on the lock screen. The lock screen will display user names at the bottom. Select the user name of the restricted profile, then unlock the screen using the PIN, password, or pattern you set.

9. If you access the app drawer, you can see that only those apps you selected for the profile will appear. These are the only apps your child can access.

Please follow this link for more detailed information:

[androidcommunity.com/how-to-set-up-parental-controls-on-android-20160530/]

Parental Controls for Television

To restrict channel and content selection, you can check with your cable or dish network provider. Usually, they will have controls available on their website to monitor and control access to programming. Unfortunately, they are currently unable to provide any type of control for time spent viewing. My best suggestion is BOB - Screen Time Manager - Manage Your TV Time & Video Game Time. This is a low-cost device you can use to restrict the amount of time your child can use the television. You can purchase it from Amazon or other outlets. Here is a list of its main features:

- Manage the time your children spend watching TV and playing video games. End the constant "TURN OFF THAT TV!" battle.

- Personal PIN access for every family member (up to 6 child accounts and 1 parent master account).

- Weekly or daily time management. Time reporting for every user.

- Time-period blocking to prevent device use at certain times of the day. (Up to five blocks per user for any or all days of the week. Maximum of 35 blocks per user per week.)

- Quickly add bonus time or remove time from any user without changing their regular allotment.

Vital Online Security Lessons for Parents and Their Tech-Savvy Kids

As a parent, one of your most important jobs is to pass along the wisdom you have accumulated to your children. From how to handle finances to how to drive, you have a lot of information to pass on. The knowledge you impart will help your kids grow into well-prepared and emotionally stable adults.

But what do you do when your kids' knowledge eclipses your own in specific areas? Chances are, your kids know as much as you do about technology—perhaps even more. How do you navigate the tricky waters of technological security and give your kids the ammunition they need to fight back against the bad guys?

One of the best things you can do is learn as much as you can about the world of technology and the places your kids inhabit online. You probably know about Facebook, but what about Snapchat? Learning as much as you can about the latest social media sites is one of the best ways to protect yourself and your offspring.

Once you know where your kids are going online and have learned as much as you can about the sites they typically visit, it's important to sit them down and have a serious discussion about the nature of the web and the security precautions they should be taking. It's never too early to start teaching your kids about online risks and how to avoid them.

Your Online Words are There Forever. Your Online Words are There Forever. One of the most important lessons parents can impart to their kids is the permanent nature of the Internet and online communications. Even if your kids favor apps like Snapchat, where conversations supposedly disappear after a few seconds, that information still exists–and it can be recovered.

If you really want to drive this message home, do a bit of digging and find something you once said online. It doesn't have to be anything embarrassing or earth-shattering, but you can use that years-old post to show your kids how the words they type today will live on forever in cyberspace. At the very least it might give them pause when they start to respond to a friend's post or join in an online bullying session.

You Can Be Anyone Online. Chances are, your kids already know this on some level, but it's essential to reinforce the fact that it's extremely easy to create a false identity online. Whether the impetus behind that false identity is evil or just good fun, the fact that it's so easy to pose as someone else is something every web user, no matter what their age, needs to understand and take seriously.

If you want to drive this lesson home, you can start by going to a random website and signing up. Even if the site does ask for an age or birth date, chances are there's not even a hint of verification in sight. This alone may not be enough to convince your kids, but it's a good first step.

Privacy Matters. It's easy to think of privacy as a mere afterthought online, but it's up to parents to stress and reinforce the importance of keeping passwords protected, keeping their computers, tablets, and phones updated, and reading privacy policies carefully. The simple fact is that privacy matters online and ignoring those privacy settings can be dangerous.

Whether you sit down with your kids and go over a sample privacy policy or share news about the latest security breach online, there are plenty of ways to teach the importance of privacy. It may take a while and a bit of repetition, but over time those lessons will begin to sink in.

Oversharing Can Be Dangerous. Studies have shown that modern children are much more comfortable sharing details of their private lives than young people just a generation ago. Sites such as Twitter, Facebook, Snapchat, Instagram and others are centered on sharing, so it's up to parents to teach the lessons of oversharing and how dangerous it can be.

Oversharing may be rampant online, but that doesn't mean your kids must participate. Whether you put an outright ban on sharing certain information, such as home addresses and the name of their school, or make helpful suggestions, stopping oversharing is one of the best ways to protect your privacy and make your kids more secure online.

It's not always easy to get kids to take online security seriously. After all, they were born into a wired world, and they have never known a place where smartphones and Facebook didn't exist. Even so, as a parent, it's your job to teach these valuable life lessons, and you need to take every opportunity to reinforce that information.

Finally, be a good role model. If you and your child are on social media, they can see your posts too. Respect their boundaries and don't comment too frequently on their posts. Also, make sure that you don't post anything that's inappropriate for your child to see.

Here are a few resources to help you with this most challenging project:

- **Common Sense Media** is a nonprofit organization with lots of valuable information for parents regarding appropriate content for children in including television, movies, apps, and video games. [commonsensemedia.org]

  PLEASE BE SURE TO VISIT THIS WEBSITE AND SUBSCRIBE TO THEIR NEWSLETTER.

- *Talking to Kids and Teens About Social Media and Sexting - Tips* from the American Academy of Pediatrics [aap.org/en-us/about-the-aap/aap-press-room/news-features-and-safety-tips/Pages/Talking-to-Kids-and-Teens-About-Social-Media-and-Sexting.aspx]

- *How to Make a Family Media Use Plan* [healthychildren.org/English/family-life/Media/Pages/How-to-Make-a-Family-Media-Use-Plan.aspx]

- *NetSmartz* is a nonprofit organization providing solid information for parents on cyber safety including cyberbullying, texting, chat, social media use and online predators. [netsmartz.org/InternetSafety]

CHAPTER 18

Getting Your Family Organized & Working Together

WE'VE COVERED A LOT of territory so far. I wouldn't be surprised if you feel somewhat overwhelmed by the suggestions I've provided. In any setting, whether that's at home, work or school, the key to success is good organization. By organizing your day and your home, you'll be able to implement the suggestions for increasing the time you spend together as a family, with your children one-on-one, with your spouse, and finally, yourself.

I'm going to briefly cover the significance of routines in the lives of children as well as offer a few suggestions for getting the morning off to a good start for the entire family. This is probably the most difficult time of the day for many families. I'll also include a few suggestions for organizing your living quarters. Finally, I'll provide some tips on teaching and motivating your children to share responsibilities around the home.

The Importance of a Regular Routine to Your Child

Regular schedules provide the day with a structure that gives a sense of order to a young child's world. Although predictability can be tiresome for adults, children thrive on repetition and routine. Schedules begin from the first days of life. Babies especially need regular sleep and meal programs, and even routines leading up to those activities.

As they get older, when a child knows what is going to happen and who is going to be there, it allows them to think and feel more independently, as well as feel more safe and secure. A disrupted routine can set a child off and cause them to feel insecure and irritable.

Regardless of how exhausted you or your children may feel, don't be tempted to skip winding down from the day. This is part of a nighttime ritual and allows both the child and parent to decompress after a busy day. It also helps bedtime go more smoothly. This is usually the time of day when a parent and child can spend some quality time together, so fight the urge to start the laundry or do the dishes until after your child has gone to bed. If this isn't possible, consider trading off these duties with your spouse each night to ensure your child has quality time with each parent on a regular basis. Take the time to find out what wind-down strategy works best for your child. Some children are energized instead of relaxed by a warm bath, so if that's the case with your child, bath time should wait for a different time of day. Whatever routine you settle on, make it quiet, relaxing and tranquil for everyone.

Though routines are important, there should be some room to be flexible as well. You might be out late at night on a family outing, have unexpected company show up which may result in a skipped meal, or nap in the car while running errands in the evening. In these instances, it's essential for you to keep your cool. If you express frustration or anger about disrupting the routine, your child will as well. Prepare children for such unexpected events and show them that although it can happen from time to time, the routine will return the next day.

How to Make Your Mornings Go More Smoothly

Early Morning is Too Late. If you're seeking to start the day off on the right foot, don't wait until the wee hours of dawn to take your first step. The night before is the most appropriate, efficient time to launch a new day.

- Make lunch ahead of time. To avoid soggy sandwiches, you can prepare the fillings and toppings in advance and then assemble it all in the morning. Fruit slices and veggie sticks can be packed in airtight containers beforehand.

- School bags should be fully packed before going to bed, including all homework and signed permission slips.

- Arrange and match all clothing, whether that is socks or hairbands, the night before. This habit prevents last-minute panic attacks upon discovering an empty drawer.

- If your gas tank is getting low, don't wait until you drive carpool to fill up. There's never time to spare on the way to school.

- Do your shoes seem to go for a stroll in the middle of the night? The case of the disappearing shoe is common. Always set shoes in a prominent and natural place, such as next to the front door, or on the floor of your closet.

- Go to bed on time. To have energy and patience for the upcoming day, both children and adults require enough hours of shut-eye.

Be Alarmed! No matter how reliable you feel your internal clock is, alarm clocks are still essential. Purchase a personal alarm clock for all family members and set it for the same minute. Whether it's a digital display with purple glitter or a vintage stainless-steel bell, allowing children to select their preference can encourage them to react positively when the alarm sounds.

Let your family democratically debate and decide the ideal wake-up time. This magic hour must be written in stone and not be snooze-able! Remember to allocate more time than you may expect, for there are always unpredictable delays.

Make a Plan. Everyone, especially children, thrives on the comforts of a routine. In general, self-esteem and confidence are bolstered when expectations are clear, and goals are achievable. Once your children's feet hit the floor, they should be able to slide smoothly into their next move.

Outline the morning schedule during a family meeting. A plan generated through teamwork is more motivating than a mandate, as no one feels that they're coerced into following someone else's ideas.

Tasks should be age-appropriate. Encourage independence whenever possible, and you'll find your mornings much quieter, not continuously punctuated by, "Can someone help me?"

List, laminate and hang up the morning itinerary, leaving nothing out. Even the most obvious jobs, such as, "Wake up and get dressed," should be posted for all to see. This will save you from chasing your kids around and shouting out reminder commands.

Make Mornings Fun. Kids love to play games. You can transform the entire morning into a race, with each family member competing for the best time or racing against the clock, setting time limits for finishing specific tasks. The winner should receive a cool prize.

Keep Focus. Concentrate on your morning itinerary and avoid distractions. School mornings aren't the time to finish the last chapter of that book or to add the final strokes to your landscape painting. Also, don't get bogged down in any complicated or heavy, emotional discussions. Push these off until evening.

Breakfast in a Snap. Breakfast should be as effortless and straightforward as possible, while still serving up nutrition that will jumpstart the day. Whole-grain cereals and milk, protein bars or yogurt topped with fruit and granola are all tasty, satisfying options that are easy to put together. Foods that demand more attention or preparation should be made in advance.

Mornings are a time to transition from sleep hours into an activity-filled day. Changing modes can be hard for anyone—even implementing the tips mentioned above can be challenging. Why not give these ideas a whirl in advance? Pretend its morning and try out your routine when you're not caught up in the frenzy of school mornings. Although practice may not make the mornings perfect, it's sure to help your family get through the morning and out the door.

Hopefully, these suggestions will help you to establish a set of routines that make life easier for the whole family. Of course, the family meeting is the best time to discuss the need for routine and discuss ideas that will work best for your family.

Organizing Your Home for Success

There is a relationship between a clean, well-organized home and the educational and financial success of the children who grew up there. In a study conducted by three university sociologists, the findings were that children completed more schooling, and earned a higher salary in clean and well-organized homes than in "not very clean to dirty" homes.

One long-term benefit of having an orderly home is that children learn this while they're growing up under their parents' influence. It's a skill that can be applied as they move on to their teenage years, make the transition to college and, ultimately, their own homes, whether they live alone, with friends, or with their own families.

Underlying our culture is a mentality concerning the collection and retention of material possessions. Because many of us either experienced or are children of people who lived through the Great Depression, we have been schooled in the practice of stockpiling possessions and retaining items whether or not they are useful or necessary.

With this in mind, what are concerned parents to do? After all, families have so much to organize, as every member of the family has both visible and non-visible aspects of their lives which require organization. The visible objects may be easier to deal with, simply because they're visible; these are clothing, work/school supplies, hobbies, toys, and food. But that is not all! Each member of the family also has responsibilities, relationships both inside and outside of the home, and limitations on their skills and time. Mix these variables, and you have the equivalent of a juggling act that takes many years of practice to keep moving smoothly.

The study, "As Ye Sweep, So Shall Ye Reap," was written by Jeanne Brooks-Gunn (Columbia University), Greg Duncan (Northwestern University) and Rachel Dunifon (University of Michigan). It was published in the May 2001 issue of the *American Economic Review*.

The first step to take when you want to get your family organized for success is to purge what is no longer useful. Things that you're not using are in the way! These items form a barrier between your family members and their successful lives. Many children have too many possessions crammed into their closets, drawers, and all over their rooms. Time spent working with the family to weed out unwanted and unneeded excess in their bedrooms is productive. Your children probably have more books, clothing, and toys than they need or want, so help them to sort through it all.

One way to appeal to children to weed out such articles is to explain that other people need and can use what they don't: children who have no books of their own, very few toys, or a limited selection of clothing from which to choose. There are three significant benefits of this activity. First, your child has a sense of contributing to another person. Secondly, this creates some space for navigating more freely in his own room. Thirdly, you teach the lesson that it's alright to get rid of things.

Most of us are so busy with our lives that we don't take the time to implement this step. Make and keep an appointment with yourselves to accomplish this task. Perhaps you can devote the first day of a vacation to the effort–the approach of a child's birthday could be a benchmark you will use–the beginning or end of a school year is an ideal time. When you do it is not nearly as important as doing it!

With permission from professional organizer and author Kathy Waddill, here are a few of the steps that she includes in the approach she recommends in her book, *The Organizing Sourcebook: Nine Strategies for Organizing Your Life*.

Design the System That Fits Your Own Life. Design the system that fits your own life. There isn't a right or wrong way to be organized in your home. Determining how to get organized takes some thought, though. What are the activities in which your family members are involved? By placing the toys, games, arts and crafts supplies, sports equipment, and homework resources at or near the places where they're used, you'll save yourself from a lot of extra effort having to pick up the trails of toy parts, game pieces, crochet hooks, sneakers, and markers that run throughout the house.

Containers are key. Here's a concept to which many people are finally catching on: place all parts of activities into containers. The see-through plastic variety is particularly useful, as you and your children will be able to see the contents before you even move the container from its location. The proper containers are also helpful in developing responsibility in young children. Assign them with the task of cleaning up when they've completed their time with the activity. It's easy for them to see on their own if they've accomplished the job: either all the parts are in the container, or they're not!

Use labels. Labeling is a tool with two uses for families, as labels promote literacy as well as organizational skills. Most important in the process of labeling is that the children be involved. That way, they get to use the words that are most meaningful to them—an integral part of making a system that will be useful for them. For young children who cannot yet read, you may either draw or cut out pictures; this is a pre-reading skill because you teach that there is a relationship between a symbol and its meaning. There's help if you need it! If you need assistance getting organized, you're not alone. More than one thousand members of the National Association of Professional Organizers (NAPO) are ready to aid you in accomplishing your goals. Founded in 1985, this organization has chapters and individual members all over the United States and in several other countries. [napo.net]

Helping Kids Learn Responsibility

It's imperative for children and teens to learn to share responsibilities in the home. Most toddlers want to mimic the chores you do—that's why we buy them toy kitchens, cleaning appliances, and toolkits. Introducing responsibility early on helps them to feel like a part of the family and to feel good about their accomplishments. Older children and teens may resist a bit as this is sometimes their nature during these stages of development; but again, they'll feel better about themselves when you encourage them to share in the responsibilities of keeping the home running smoothly.

Family meetings are the best setting to discuss the chores necessary around the home. Ask your children how they feel they can help best. Taking care of their bedroom is not a chore but a responsibility worthy of praise and reward—the same for getting their homework done on time. Chores are tasks we perform for the good of the whole family. Simple cleaning around the house, taking care of a pet, taking out the trash, raking leaves, mowing the lawn, clearing the table, washing dishes, helping prepare meals, and helping with laundry are a few examples. Chores need to be age-appropriate. For many duties, you'll need to teach your child or teen how to accomplish the task and how to achieve the level of competence you expect. Specific days and/or times for completion of a job must also be determined.

Finally, you need to come up with a list of privileges or other rewards that can be earned by spending points. Electronic devices could be used by the hour through a "rental system" using points. Some points could convert to money for their allowance. Points could also be used for special privileges such as staying up an hour later on the weekends, going to a movie, going to a friend's house, choosing where to go for lunch or dinner at a restaurant, choosing what game to play during family fun night, and getting a new book, toy, video game, or other item. Let your child suggest rewards as well.

As with chores, discuss beforehand how the point values determine rewards. Maximum limits probably will need to be set for time spent on using electronic devices, how much allowance they can earn per week and providing a list to choose from for restaurants, movies, outings, etc.

Once you've come up with a list of responsibilities and rewards, you're ready to list them on the **Personal Responsibility Chart** provided at the end of this section. The chart is designed to make it easy for you to record earning and spending of points. You can post this at your family command center, so it's easy for everyone to see. Family meetings can also be the time for payday. This gives you an opportunity to praise extraordinary accomplishments in public. From time to time, the list will need to be evaluated and changed as a child matures and becomes able to take on more demanding tasks. Make sure you also acknowledge from time to time the chores completed by the adults in the family as well, so children are aware that everyone in the family is doing their part. Sorry, no points for adults.

CHAPTER 19
Homework / School Issues

WITH THE COMPETITIVE, NOT to mention stressful, academic environment today, more and more kids are experiencing difficulty keeping up with the demands of the school. Experts say that one of the primary reasons why students, especially the younger ones, get tired or bored is that they are given lots of assignments without knowing where to get help with their homework. At home, it is parents who take on the responsibility of helping their children with assignments.

Helping Kids Cope with Homework

Doing homework is one of the things children often hate to do. Most of the time, they put off finishing their homework because they think it's a tiresome task that will take them hours to complete. Kids naturally want to have fun—they'll choose playing games over doing tedious assignments any day. Many things compete for their attention, from TV shows and video games to mobile phones and the Internet. To the eyes of children, there are numerous other more interesting things than homework. Their idea of fun is not racking their brains over math problems or spelling assignments.

As a parent, your role is crucial in shaping your child's study and homework habits. You want him to develop good study habits and do his homework diligently. However, continually punishing, nagging, or arguing with your stubborn kid rarely works in the long term, and such methods only cause more resistance, whining, and complaints. Follow the suggestions below to set up a homework routine and encourage your child to finish his assignments satisfactorily every time.

Establish a Homework Routine on the First Day of School. Establish a homework routine on the first day of school. Creating a regular homework routine that involves when and where assignments need to completion is essential. Students greatly benefit from clear structures for completing homework. It's often easier to accomplish tasks when they're used to specific routines.

If possible, implement a homework routine as soon as school starts. However, it's not yet too late even if it's halfway through the school year, as long as you're consistent with your daily setup. After a few weeks, the routine will become embedded in your child's everyday activities, and he will naturally get used to doing his homework.

A solid homework routine reflects your child's unique learning style. Students with weakness in being focused and attentive usually work best when they spend only up to 15 minutes on a particular subject, move on to the next for another 15 minutes, and then go back to the previous assignment. This is a more productive approach than forcing your child to work continuously on the same homework.

On the other hand, some students accomplish things better when they spend half an hour on homework, take a short break to eat snacks or play, and go back to completing the assignment. Different approaches tailored to a student's individual needs are necessary. To find out which homework routine is best for your child, talk to him and ask about his preferences. You may also try out several approaches and observe which ones produce the best results.

Find a Suitable Space in Your Home Where Your Child Can Do Homework. The right location depends on your child's preferences. Some kids find it comfortable to work in their rooms, where the quiet ambiance promotes concentration. Others are easily distracted by playthings in their bedroom, so are likely to perform better at a location with fewer distractions, such as the dining room table. Some children love to sprawl out on the living room floor when doing homework.

Ask your child about where he'll feel most relaxed to accomplish school assignments. Ideally, the location should be quiet, clean, and free of distraction, allowing your child to stay focused. The homework space should also be comfortable and inviting. If it's always noisy at home, suggest the use of noise-canceling headphones. If your child finds it more relaxing to listen to mellow music, try playing music in the background. To pick the right location, discuss the pros and cons of available choices. It's important to choose an area both you and your child will enjoy.

Create a Homework Center. After identifying the location most conducive to completing homework, the next step is to set it up as a homework center. Ensure that the workspace is roomy enough to accommodate all necessary materials for doing assignments. Find out the types of supplies your child typically uses, and provide them, including pencils, pens, papers, colored markers, and rulers. A dictionary, thesaurus, and calculator may also be necessary.

Depending on the grade level and particular needs of your child, you may also let him use a computer or laptop. Additionally, buy a portable crate to store supplies if the homework center serves other purposes. Place a bulletin board where you can hang a monthly calendar for keeping track of long-term assignments.

Allow your child to participate in designing the homework center. Let him share his creativity in improving the place, so he can feel more comfortable and excited to do assignments in his chosen area. However, make sure the homework center doesn't become excessively cluttered with unnecessary materials. Ban video game consoles, mobile devices, and other distractions until homework is done or until break time.

Allow your child to participate in designing the homework center. Let him share his creativity in improving the space, so he can feel more comfortable and excited to do assignments in his chosen area. However, make sure the homework center doesn't become excessively cluttered with unnecessary materials. Ban video game consoles, mobile devices, and other distractions until the homework completion or until break time.

Choose a Homework Time. It's essential to establish a particular time for doing homework every day. Your child should be able to get used to this schedule until it becomes a regular daily routine. Some students need one or two hours of a break after school to have a snack and enjoy some exercise, while others perform better when starting homework immediately upon arriving home. Again, discuss this with your child, and talk about the advantages and disadvantages of different homework periods.

Usually, the best time to tackle homework is before dinner. It's also good to do homework after dinner when children feel full and have replenished their energy levels. However, avoid doing assignments later in the evening, because your child may feel too exhausted to think clearly.

Set a Regular Homework Session. At the start of a homework session, sit alongside your child and draw up a schedule for the day. It's best to create a daily homework planner that specifies the amount of time allotted for each assignment. It's your role to review each assignment and ensure that your child understands everything. Let him estimate the amount of time he needs to complete each one. Ask which one he'd like to do first and find out if he needs help with anything. This will allow you to adjust the time of completing homework accordingly.

Include Breaks. Working on assignments continuously can quickly drain your child physically and mentally. Let him decide when he'd like to take a break and include his chosen break periods in the daily homework schedule. Some kids want to take a break at particular time intervals, such as every 15 minutes or every half an hour, while others prefer to take a break once they finish an assignment. Identify the length of each break period and what your child can do during the break, such as having a snack, watching TV, or playing a game.

Convey Your Expectations and Set Limits. When setting limits and creating rules, tell your child that homework should be done at the same time and same area every day. Moreover, let your child know what you expect from him. You can establish mutually agreed written expectations to make everything clear from the start.

Offer rewards. Mark your homework calendar for each day of successful completion of assignments and offer rewards and incentives on certain days. For example, you may want to create a mystery box of treats and toys and allow your child to grab inside the box a few times a week. Other possible incentives include access to electronics, playtime with friends, or the purchase of new video games at the end of the month. This could be added to the **Personal Responsibility Chart** presented in the previous chapter on responsibility.

Organize Study and Homework Projects. Use the Homework Planner and Long- Term Homework Planner charts at the end of this section to keep track of assignments.

Teach Your Child That Studying Is More Than Just Doing Homework Assignments. One of the most misunderstood aspects of schoolwork is the difference between studying and doing homework assignments. Encourage your child to do things such as:

- Take notes as she's reading a chapter.

- Learn to skim material.

- Learn to study tables and charts.

- Learn to summarize what she has read in her own words.

- Learn to make her own flashcards for a quick review of dates, formulas, spelling words, etc.

Note-taking is a Critical Skill for Kids to Develop. Many students don't know how to take notes in those classes that require them. Some feel they must write down every word the teacher says. Others have wisely realized the value of an outline form of note-taking. Well-prepared teachers present their material in a format that lends itself to outline form note taking.

Should Notes Ever Be Rewritten? In some cases, they should be, particularly if a lot of material was covered, and the child had to write quickly—but lacks speed and organization. Rewriting notes takes time, but it can be an excellent review of the subject matter. However, rewriting notes isn't worth the time unless they are used for review and recall of valuable information.

Help Your Child to Feel Confident for Tests. Taking tests can be a traumatic experience for some students. Explain to your child that burning the midnight oil (cramming) the night before a test is not productive. It's better to get a good night's sleep. Students also need reminding that when taking a test, they should thoroughly and carefully read directions before they haphazardly start to mark their test papers. They should be advised to skip over questions for which they don't know the answers. They can always return to those if there's time. Good advice for any student before taking a test: take a deep breath, relax and dive in. Always bring an extra pencil just in case.

During a Homework Session, Watch for Signs of Frustration. No learning can take place, and little can be accomplished if the child is angry or upset over an assignment that is too long or too difficult. Teach your child how to break the task into smaller chunks. Occasionally, the parent may have to step in and halt the homework for that night, offering to write a note to the teacher explaining the situation and requesting a conference to discuss the quality and length of homework assignments.

Staying on Task. Consider using a timer if your child has difficulty staying on task. Sometimes a "beat the clock system" is effective in motivating. Let your child have a short break (10-15 minutes) in between subjects or assignments. Encourage exercise, but a short video game is okay as well.

Should Parents Help with Homework? Yes–if it's productive to do so, such as calling out spelling words or checking a math problem that won't prove. No–if it's something the child can handle himself and learn from the process. And help and support should always be calmly and cheerfully given. Grudging help is worse than no help at all! Read directions or check over math problems after your child has completed the work. Remember to make positive comments– you don't want your child to associate homework with fights at home.

Make Connections to Your Family's Real Life. Homework is much more meaningful when students can see a connection between what they're doing and their own lives. Look for opportunities to incorporate the topics you see them exploring into your family's daily life. If your daughter is learning fractions, hand her the pizza cutter! If your son is studying Spanish verbs, take him to an authentic Mexican restaurant and ask him to order in Spanish for the entire family! You can also talk to your children about the relationship between what they're learning and what you do in your own job so that they can see concrete evidence of the value of their studies.

Find a Healthy Balance. Homework is important, but it isn't everything. Don't let the pursuit of academic excellence take away from your child's other interests, such as athletics, music, art or community service. Children and teenagers also need unstructured time with their friends to develop critical social skills. For older teenagers, balancing homework with a part-time job can help them build independence and financial management skills that will be essential in the future. Give your children the best start possible by finding a balance between homework and all of the other things that will allow them to grow into happy, healthy, well-rounded adults.

With a proper homework center, a regular schedule, and clear rules, you'll be able to reinforce a positive and long-lasting habit. Make sure to communicate clearly and try to make homework a fun experience rather than a chore. By working alongside your child and guiding him well, you can encourage him to finish his homework willingly every day.

Here are few online resources for help with homework

- **Homework Help** (provides tips and useful tools for parents, children and teens). Provided by Kids Health, a nonprofit organization. [kidshealth.org/en/kids/center/homework.html]

- **Fact Monster** is a great source for finding information on a wide array of school subjects and topics. [factmonster.com]

- **Kahn Academy** is a fantastic resource for online tutoring via videos. It is absolutely free and recommended by teachers. It covers any topic and any level from elementary school through college. [khanacademy.org]

- **Common Sense Media:** Best for Learning: Our Recommendations for Families

  Discover the best in learning apps, games, and websites for your kids. "Best of" lists offer handpicked, carefully reviewed titles grouped by category. Topics range from skills essential to life and work in the 21st century, to traditional academic subjects, to recommendations for particular settings or types of kids. And these titles are FUN! After all, excited, engaged kids are primed for learning.

  [commonsensemedia.org/best-for-learning-lists]

Section 4 – Organization - Summary

Ideas & Recommendations for Helping your Family Get Organized

Suggestions for Getting Your Family Organized for Success through Working Together and Supporting Each Other:

1. Prepare for and hold your first family meeting using the guidelines provided in Chapter 16.

2. Use family meetings to discuss family member responsibilities and set up a plan for sharing household responsibilities. Look at the Chore Chart options as possible tools.

3. Discuss morning and afternoon routines at family meetings as needed. Use the Morning Routine and Afternoon Routine charts. You can set one up for the entire family or one for each family member.

4. Use family meetings as well as individual meetings with each child to establish homework routines. The Homework Planner may be a useful tool.

5. Find a place in your home to be the designated "Command Center." It might be a bulletin board or the side of the refrigerator. This provides a place for you to post items such as the Chore Chart, Activity Calendar, Morning Routine, and other information of value to the family.

Tools for Success: Organization

Week at Glance: This is a simple tool you can post to let everyone know what is going on. You can discuss and revise at family meetings.

Weekday Routines: This can be used to help children stay organized and keep an agreed to schedule.

Personal Responsibility Chart: This is an easy way to keep track of chores. Points could be converted to a monetary figure for allowance or could be used to earn rewards and privileges.

- Meet with your child and come up with a list of chores & responsibilities.

- Come up with a list of rewards or privileges such as renting electronics, toys for a period of time, the privilege of selecting a place to eat, watching a TV show or movie, staying up late on the weekend, etc.

- Determine points for completing tasks based on time or effort. Determine points for rewards based on frequency, expense, or fairness to other family members. Try to see that most of the points are attained for a day that there would be enough points for usual daily activities. Leftover points could be carried forward for more costly rewards.

- Update the point chart at least daily. Be sure to offer praise and thanks.

- When you feel primary goals have been attained, you could hold a graduation ceremony and just use a reminder check list and a weekly allowance and/or reasonable access to privileges.

Homework Planner: This is a simple tool to help students keep track of assignments and be able to plan study time to be able to complete all assignments on time.

Long-Term Homework Project Planner: Many kids have difficulty handling larger, long-term assignments. They often will put them off because they're unable to develop a strategy to complete the assignment.

- Parents should help them learn to break a large project into smaller, sequential steps leading to the completion of the project. For instance, if the child needs to read a 200-page book in two weeks, they could decide to read 20 pages per week day. Doing that makes it seem more doable.

- Larger written projects could be broken down to (1) select a topic, (2) look for information (if there is sufficient information, move forward, otherwise revise the topic), (3) gather information, (4) decide on the theme sentence and outline of supporting components, (5) write each of the supporting parts, (6) write a conclusion, (7) write any other required elements such a title page, bibliography, etc. Once the steps have been developed, set a timeline for each that will enable them to complete several days before the due date.

- Individual steps could be added to a Weekly Homework Planner.

Please be sure to visit parentingtoday.com/tools for PDF versions of the charts provided at the end of each section as well as additional resources, including updates, classes, and forums for parents.

Our Family Week at a Glance Week of: _____

Monday	Tuesday	Wednesday	Thursday	Friday	Saturday
					Sunday

Kids Activities

				To Do List

Dinner Plans

Special Time

Notes

Weekday Routines for _____

Morning

Activity	Time It Should Be Completed

After School

Activity	Time It Should Be Completed

Bedtime

Activity	Time It Should Be Completed

Personal Responsibility Chart for _____ Week of _____

Chore/Responsibility	Points	Monday	Tuesday	Wednesday	Thursday	Friday	Saturday	Sunday
Total Earned								
Carry Over from Day Before								
Total Spent								
Points Left								
Carry Over to Next Day								

Homework Planner For _____ Week Of _____

Subject	Monday	Tuesday	Wednesday	Thursday	Weekend

Long Term Homework Planner For _____

Class/Project	Due Date:	Completed By
Step 1		
Step 2		
Step 3		
Step 4		
Step 5		

Class/Project	Due Date:	
Step 1		
Step 2		
Step 3		
Step 4		
Step 5		

Class/Project	Due Date:	
Step 1		
Step 2		
Step 3		
Step 4		
Step 5		

CONCLUSION

How to Get Started Improving the Balance for Your Family

BALANCING ACTS ARE NOT always easy. It's hard enough for an individual to find balance in their life, so a group effort is naturally even more difficult. I hope that at least glancing through this book has sparked an interest in you to move forward with the goal of improving the balance within your family, as well as for each member.

The toughest part is to make a commitment to the goal and begin taking steps to move toward the goal ASAP. I remember hearing a motivational speaker say, "If you don't start putting what you just learned into practice immediately, it won't happen." Many well-intentioned people have spent money to go to a seminar and never taken a first step to act on the knowledge. Others of us have collections of books and CDs purchased with the excitement of making positive life changes sitting on bookshelves or packed away in boxes that have never been opened. So, I encourage you to begin taking the first step now before you set down this book.

Here are my suggestions for moving forward:

1. Decide now that this is worth doing.

2. Share your thoughts and feelings about improving balance with your spouse or partner. If they are on board, set up a meeting to share opinions and arrive at a common ground.

3. Decide on the agenda, and when you should hold your first family meeting.

4. Discuss the concept with your kids. It might be a good idea to talk about it over a meal.

5. During the first meeting, discuss ground rules and encourage participation from everyone.

6. Set a few goals.

7. Set ground rules for the use of electronics. Get your family docking station and set a date for the electronics use plan to start.

I tried to avoid getting too specific in sharing my ideas because this should be your adventure and should be in tune with your values and lifestyle. The purpose of the book is to provide you with some basic information based on sound psychology to help you to see the big picture, coupled with some suggestions on activities and interventions as a point of departure.

My best to you and your family in your journey together. I know that if you implement some of the concepts and suggestions presented here, you and your family will experience the rewards from your effort. Eventually, this will not become a new effort or project but a new way of life.

There is no better time to start the process of decreasing screen time while increasing family fun, fitness and connectedness than this very moment.

"The most difficult thing is the decision to act, the rest is merely tenacity. The fears are paper tigers. You can do anything you decide to do. You can act to change and control your life; and the procedure, the process is its own reward." – Amelia Earhart

RESOURCES

Selected resources including additional information and tools (products) to help you implement your plan to build a Well-Balanced Family.

Chapter 5 – The Importance of Play in the Lives of Children & Families

Websites

The Importance of Play in Promoting Healthy Child Development and Maintaining Strong (American Academy of Pediatrics) [pediatrics. aappublications.org/content/119/1/182]

The Importance of Play: Activities for Children (childaction.org) [pathways. org/news/articles/importance-of-play-in-childrens-development/]

Books

Brown, SL. Play, *How it Shapes the Brain, Opens the Imagination, and Invigorates the Soul*. Penguin; 2009.

Elkind, D. *The Power of Play: Learning What Comes Naturally*. Da Capro Press; 2007

Cohen, LJ. *Playful Parenting: An Exciting New Approach to Raising Children That Will Help You Nurture Close Connections, Solve Behavior Problems, and Encourage Confidence*.

Random House; 2001.

Chapter 6 – Family Traditions & Family Activities

<u>Websites</u>

60+ Family Tradition Ideas (The Art of Manliness)
[artofmanliness.com/articles/60-family-tradition-ideas/]
Your Family Rituals (American Academy of Pediatrics)
[healthychildren.org/English/family-life/family-dynamics/Pages/Your-Family-Rituals.aspx]

<u>Books</u>

St Clair-Jackson, J (Editor) *Family Traditions for a Fast-Paced World: Simple Everyday Rituals for Comfort and Connectio*n. Amberwood Press; 2016
Cox, M. <u>The Book of New Family Traditions: How to Create Great Rituals for Holidays and Every Day</u>. Running Press; 2012

Chapter 7 – Connecting with Your Kids

<u>Websites</u>

5 Attachment-Based Activities to Strengthen Parent-Child Relationships (Psych Central)
[pro.psychcentral.com/child-therapist/2014/08/5-attachment-based-activities-to-strengthen-parent-child-relationships/]
<u>78 Parent Child Activities</u> (Life Learning Today)
[lifelearningtoday.com/2007/05/20/78-parent-child-activities-free-download/]
Relationship-Building Exercises for Teens & Parents (Our Everyday Life)
[oureverydaylife.com/relationshipbuilding-exercises-teens-parents-12153.html]

<u>Books</u>

Gopnik, A. *The Gardener and the Carpenter: What the New Science of Child Development Tells Us About the Relationship Between Parents and Children.* Farrar, Straus and Giroux; 2016

Siegel, D. & Payne-Bryson, T. *The Whole-Brain Child: 12 Revolutionary Strategies to Nurture Your Child's Developing Mind.* Bantam Books; 2012

Chapter 9 – Family Reading Time

Websites
Reading Rockets: Launching Young Readers Reading Aloud with Children of All Ages
[readingrockets.org/launching]
Books
Trelease J. The Read-aloud Handbook. Penguin; 2013.
Fox M, Horacek J. Reading Magic, Why Reading Aloud to Our Children Will Change Their Lives Forever. Houghton Mifflin Harcourt; 2008.
Tools
Books to Read Aloud to Children (a list at Amazon.com)
Reading Horizons – Home-based reading program to improve reading comprehension and reading skills [athome.readinghorizons.com/method]

Chapter 10 – Supportive Communication

Books
Faber A, Mazlish E, Faber J. *How to Talk So Kids Will Listen & Listen So Kids Will Talk.* Simon and Schuster; 2012.
Farber, J. & King, J. *How to Talk So Little Kids Will Listen: A Survival Guide to Life with Children Ages 2-7.* Scribner; 2017
Faber A, Mazlish E. How to Talk so Teens Will Listen and Listen so Teens Will. Harper Collins; 2006.

Chapter 11 – Motivation and Encouragement

Websites
Encouraging & Praising Kids (Australian Early Childhood Initiative)
[kidsmatter.edu.au/mental-health-matters/social-and-emotional-learning/ motivation-and-praise-encourage]

Motivation -- Helping Your Child Through Early Adolescence (U.S.
Department of Education)
[www2.ed.gov/parents/academic/help/adolescence/partx4.html]
The 7 Secrets of Motivating Teenagers (Understanding Teens)
[understandingteenagers.com.au/blog/
the-7-secrets-of-motivating-teenagers/]

Books
Covey S. *The 7 Habits of Highly Effective Families*. Macmillan; 1998.
Covey S. *The 7 Habits of Happy Kids*. Simon and Schuster; 2008.
Covey S. The 7 Habits of Highly Effective Teens, Personal Workbook.
Turtleback; 2004.

Chapter 12 – Handling Conflicts

Websites
Resolving Family Conflicts (Clemson University)
[nasdonline.org/1444/d001244/resolving-family-conflicts.html]
6 Steps for Resolving Conflict in Marriage (Family Life)
[familylife.com/articles/topics/marriage/staying-married/
resolving-conflict/6-steps-for-resolving-conflict-in-marriage/]
Teaching Children to Resolve Conflict Respectfully (Parenting Exchange)
[easternflorida.edu/community-resources/child-development-centers/parent-
resource-library/documents/teaching-kids-to-resolve-conflicts-respectfully.
pdf]
Conflict Management with Teenagers (Raising Children Network, Australia)
[raisingchildren.net.au/articles/conflict_management_teenagers.html]

Books
Faber A, Mazlish E. *Siblings Without Rivalry, How to Help Your Children Live
Together So You Can Live Too.* Piccadilly Press; 1999.

Brown ND. *Ending the Parent-teen Control Battle, Resolve the Power Struggle and Build Trust, Responsibility, and Respect.* New Harbinger Publications; 2016.

Robinson J. Communication Miracles for Couples, Easy and Effective Tools to Create More Love and Less Conflict. Conari Press; 2012.

Chapter 13 – Family Fitness

Websites
Play Games Online for Exercise and Healthy Eating (USDA)
[healthyeating.org/Healthy-Kids/Kids-Games-Activities]
Make Physical Activity a Part of Your Family's Routine (Let's Move)
[letsmove.obamawhitehouse.archives.gov/
make-physical-activity-part-your-familys-routine]
Let's Move! Family Activities (Let's Move)
[letsmove.obamawhitehouse.archives.gov/sites/letsmove.gov/files/
FamilyActivitiesAccessible.pdf]

Books
Rockwell L. *The Busy Body Book, A Kid's Guide to Fitness.* Knopf Books for Young Readers; 2012.
Weis SJ. Go Go Yoga Kids, Empower Kids for Life Through Yoga. 2016.
Lingampalli K. Teenager's Guide to Health and Fitness. Xlibris Corporation; 2013.

Tools
Exergaming Devices:
- Kinect for Xbox 360 -With multi-and single-player games that include boxing, volleyball, Kung Fu, track and field, soccer, and more, the Kinect is hands-free, using a sensor in the game console to track movement, then translate it into game play.

- PlayStation Move - Employing a camera and a motion controller remote, this gaming console offers exercise game titles for single and multi-player play, including beach volleyball, disc golf, archery, dance, table tennis, kickboxing, and more.

- <u>Nintendo Wii Fit</u> - Featuring multi- and single-player games, including skateboarding, hula, Kung Fu, skiing, dance games and more, the Wii Fit uses a balance board and remote, both of which translate real-life movement into game play.

Chapter 14 – Family Mealtime

<u>Websites</u>
Choose My Plate - Children (USDA)
[choosemyplate.gov/children]
Choose My Plate - Teens (USDA)
[choosemyplate.gov/teens]
<u>Play Games Online for Exercise and Healthy Eating</u> (USDA)
[healthyeating.org/Healthy-Kids/Kids-Games-Activities]

<u>Books</u>
Home EA. <u>Taste of Home 100 Family Meals</u>. Simon and Schuster; 2016.
Rosenstrach J. Dinner, <u>A 30-Day Plan for Mastering the Art of the Family Meal. Ballantine Books</u>; 2014.

<u>Tools</u>
Super Healthy Kids - Super Healthy Kids helps parents make fruits and vegetables simple, fun, and delicious! Ideas from our blog, recipes from our meal plans, and our Healthy Habits products help you make your kids (Super Healthy Kids!)
[superhealthykids.com/]

Chapter 15 – The Importance of a Good Night's Sleep

<u>Websites</u>
<u>Good, Sound Sleep for Your Child</u> (WebMD)
[webmd.com/children/features/good-sound-sleep-for-children]
<u>Teens and Sleep: How to Get Them to Get Enough</u> (WebMD)

[webmd.com/parenting/raising-fit-kids/recharge/features/
help-teens-get-sleep]

Books
Weissbluth M. *Healthy Sleep Habits, Happy Child, A Step-by-step Program for a Good Night's Sleep.* 2015.
M.D. DH, Whiteley C. *Snooze. or Lose! 10 "No-War" Ways to Improve Your Teen's Sleep Habits.* Joseph Henry Press; 2006.

Tools
Indigo Dreams: Relaxation and Stress Management Bedtime Stories for Children, Improve Sleep, Manage Stress and Anxiety [Audio CD]
Indigo Teen Dreams: 2 CD Set Designed to Decrease Stress, Anger, Anxiety while Increasing Self-Esteem and Self-Awareness [Audio CD]

Chapter 16 – Family Meetings

Websites
10 Tips for Holding a Family Meeting (Psychology Today)
[psychologytoday.com/us/blog/
emotional-fitness/201209/10-tips-holding-family-meeting]
How to Plan and Lead a Weekly Family Meeting (The Art of Manliness)
[artofmanliness.com/articles/creating-a-positive-family-culture-how-to-plan-and-lead-a-weekly-family-meeting/]

Chapter 17 – Managing Screen Time and Cyber Safety

Websites
Common Sense Media is a nonprofit organization with lots of valuable information for parents regarding appropriate content for children in including television, movies, apps, and video games. [commonsensemedia.org]
PLEASE BE SURE TO VISIT THIS WEBSITE AND SUBSCRIBE TO THEIR NEWSLETTER.

Parent's Guide – Internet Safety
[internetsafety101.org/parentsguidetosocialmedia]
Screen Time and Children — How to Guide Your Child (Mayo Clinic)
[mayoclinic.org/healthy-lifestyle/childrens-health/in-depth/screen-time/art-20047952]
Where We Stand: Screen Time (American Academy of Pediatrics)
[healthychildren.org/English/family-life/Media/Pages/Where-We-Stand-TV-Viewing-Time.aspx]
Video Game Addiction—Is it Real? (National Institute of Health)
[teens.drugabuse.gov/blog/post/video-game-addiction-is-it-real]

Books
Willard NE. *Cyber-Safe Kids, Cyber-Savvy Teens, Helping Young People Learn To Use the Internet Safely and Responsibly*. John Wiley & Sons; 2007.
Kutscher, ML. *Digital Kids: How to Balance Screen Time, and Why It Matters*. Jessica Kingsley Publishers; 2017
Dunckley, VL. Reset Your Child's Brain, A Four-Week Plan to End Meltdowns, Raise Grades, and Boost Social Skills by Reversing the Effects of Electronic Screen-Time. New World Library; 2015.
Citro A. 150+ Screen-Free Activities for Kids, The Very Best and Easiest Playtime Activities. Simon and Schuster; 2014.

Chapter 18 – Getting Your Family Organized & Working Together

Websites
How to Organize Your Family (Wiki How)
[wikihow.com/Organize-Your-Family]
How to Organize Your Family Chaos with the Help of Technology (Life Hacker)
[lifehacker.com/how-to-organize-your-family-chaos-with-the-help-of-tech-1595502673]

Books

Reyes, M. *Declutter Home: Home Organizing Methods & Exercises for Family.* Book Tier; 2015
Upton S. Building Your House, A Faithful Mom's Guide to Organizing Home and Family. 2015.

Chapter 19 – Home / School Issues

Websites

Helping Your Child with Homework (U.S. Department of Education) [www2.ed.gov/parents/academic/help/homework/partx2.html]
Helping with Homework (PBS Parents) [pbs.org/parents/education/going-to-school/supporting-your-learner/ homework-help/]

Books

Wilhelm MF. Homework Hang-Ups, Tips for Helping Your Child With Homework Demands. CreateSpace; 2014.
Kruger SW. *SOAR Study Skills, A Simple and Efficient System for Earning Better Grades in Less Time.* S O A R Learning; 2007.

> Please be sure to visit parentingtoday.com/tools for PDF versions of the charts provided at the end of each section as well as additional resources, including updates, classes, and forums for parents.

BIBLIOGRAPHY

Angier, N. (2013, November 25). The Changing American Family. *The New York Times*. Retrieved from www.nytimes.com/2013/11/26/health/families. html

Beck, M.E. (2007). Dinner preparation in the modern United States. *British Food Journal* 109(7):531- 547.

Brown, S. L. (2009). Play: How it shapes the brain, opens the imagination, and invigorates the soul. Penguin.

Carvalho, J., Fonseca, G., Francisco, R., Bacigalupe, G., & Relvas, A. P. (2016). Information and Communication Technologies and Family: Patterns of Use, Life Cycle and Family Dynamics. *Journal of Psychology & Psychotherapy, 2016*.

Carvalho, J., Francisco, R., & Relvas, A. P. (2015). Family functioning and information and communication technologies: How do they relate? A literature review. *Computers in Human Behavior, 45*, 99–108.

Dewar, G. (2008). The cognitive benefits of play: Effects on the learning brain. Parenting Science. Retrieved from http://www.parentingscience.com/ benefits-of-play.html.

Dickstein, S. (2002). Family routines and rituals–The importance of family functioning: Comment on the special section., *16*(4), 441–444

Ginsburg, K. R., & others. (2007). The importance of play in promoting healthy child development and maintaining strong parent-child bonds, *119*(1), 182–191.

Gray, P. (2011). The decline of play and the rise of psychopathology in children and adolescents. *American Journal of Play*, *3*(4), 443-463.

Hill, D. A., Nusheen Reid Chassiakos, Yolanda (Linda) Cross, Corinn Hutchinson, Jeffrey Levine, Alanna Boyd, Rhea Mendelson, Robert Moreno, Megan Swanson, Wendy Sue (Ed.). (2016). Media and Young Minds. *Pediatrics*

Huisman, S., Edwards, A., Catapano, S., & others. (2012). The impact of technology on families, (II-1), 44–62.

Hutton, J. S., Horowitz-Kraus, T., Mendelsohn, A. L., DeWitt, T., & Holland, S. K. (2015). Home Reading Environment and Brain Activation in Preschool Children Listening to Stories. *Pediatrics*, *136*(3), 466

Jelenchick, L. A., Eickhoff, J., Christakis, D. A., Brown, R. L., Zhang, C., Benson, M., & Moreno, M. A. (2014). The Problematic and Risky Internet Use Screening Scale (PRIUSS) for Adolescents and Young Adults: Scale Development and Refinement. *Computers in Human Behavior*, *35*.

Kabali, H. K., Irigoyen, M. M., Nunez-Davis, R., Budacki, J. G., Mohanty, S. H., Leister, K. P., & Bonner, R. L. (2015). Exposure and use of mobile media devices by young children. *Pediatrics*, 2015.

Klein, W., Graesch, A. P. & Izquierdo, C. (2009). Children and chores: A mixed-methods study of children's household work in Los Angeles families. *Anthropology of Work Review* 30(3): 98-109.

Klein, W., Izquierdo, C. & Bradbury, T. (2007). Working relationships: communicative patterns and strategies among couples in everyday life. *Qualitative Methods in Psychology* 4:29-47.

Kremer-Sadlik, T. & Kim, J. L. (2007). Lessons from sports: Children's socialization to values through family interaction during sports activities. *Discourse & Society* 18(1):35-52.

Kremer-Sadlik, T. & Paugh, A. (2007). Everyday moments: Finding 'quality time' in American working families. *Time & Society* 16(2/3):287-308.

Lezin, N., Rolleri, L., Bean, S. & Taylor, J. (2004). Parent-child connectedness: Implications for research, interventions and positive impacts on adolescent health. Santa Cruz, CA: ETR Associates.

Lauricella, A. R., Wartella, E., & Rideout, V. J. (2015). Young children's screen time: The complex role of parent and child factors. *Journal of Applied Developmental Psychology, 36*, 11–17.

Neumann, M. M. (2015). Young children and screen time: Creating a mindful approach to digital technology. *Australian Educational Computing, 30*(2).

Ochs, E., Shohet, M., Campos, B. & Beck, M. (2010). Coming together for dinner: A study of working families. In K. Christensen & B. Schneider (Eds.), *Workplace Flexibility: Realigning 20th Century Jobs to 21st Century Workforce*, pg. 57-70. Ithaca, NY: Cornell University Press.

Ochs, E. & Izquierdo, C. (2009). Responsibility in childhood: Three developmental trajectories. *Ethos* 37(4): 391-413.

Reid Chassiakos, Y. (Linda), Radesky, J., Christakis, D., Moreno, M. A., & Cross, C. (2016). Children and Adolescents and Digital Media. *Pediatrics*.

ABOUT THE AUTHOR

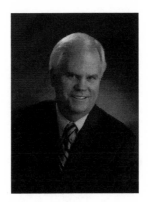

ROBERT MYERS, PHD IS a child psychologist with over 35 years of clinical experience. He is Associate Clinical Professor of Psychiatry and Human Behavior at the UC Irvine School of Medicine. Dr Myers also provides parent education through public speaking and media appearances. He is the founder of a popular website for parents, Child Development Institute at <u>www.child-developmentinfo.com</u>. Robert Myers lives in Orange, CA with his wife, Pam. They were married in 1971 and have two adult children. He likes to listen to music and go to concerts, travel to new places, photography, and go hiking in the local mountains. Most of all he likes to spend time with his family, especially playing board games and having fun.